Jacek Jackiewicz
Robert Bock

Colour profiles:
Jacek Jackiewicz

Assembly Ships
of the Mighty Eighth

Published in Poland in 2025
by STRATUS s.j.
Żeromskiego 6A
27-600 Sandomierz, Poland
e-mail: office@mmpbooks.biz
for
Mushroom Model Publications,
e-mail: rogerw@mmpbooks.biz
© 2025 Mushroom Model Publications.
http://www.mmpbooks.biz

All rights reserved. Apart from any fair dealing for the purpose of private study, research, criticism or review, as permitted under the Copyright, Design and Patents Act, 1988, no part of this publication may be reproduced, stored in a retrieval system, or transmitted in any form or by any means, electronic, electrical, chemical, mechanical, optical, photocopying, recording or otherwise, without prior written permission. All enquiries should be addressed to the publisher.

ISBN 978-83-67227-85-8

Editor in chief
Roger Wallsgrove

Editorial Team
Robert Pęczkowski
Artur Juszczak

Text and research
Jacek Jackiewicz
Robert Bock

Colour profiles
Jacek Jackiewicz

DTP
Stratus sp. j.

PRINTED IN POLAND

AD	CBW	BG	Type	Aircraft	Serial	Name	Dates
1st AD	1st CBW	91st BG	AS	none			
			FM	P-51	unkn.		
		381st BG	AS	B-17 E	41-9043	Little Rock-ette (ex – Peggy D)	? – 5.45
			FM	?	?		
		398th BG	AS	none			
			FM	?			
	40th CBW	92nd BG	AS	none			
			FM	P-47 D-5-RE	42-8522		
		305th BG	AS	none			
			FM	P-47 D-15-RE	42-75621		
		306th BG	AS	none			
			FM	P-47 D-1-RE	42-7938		
	41st CBW	303rd BG	AS	B-17 E	41-9020	Tugboat Annie (ex – Phillys)	6.44 – 7.44
			AS	B-17 F-80-BO	42-29947	Wabash Cannonball	9.44 – 5.45
			FM	P-47 D-5-RE	42-8567		
			FM	P-47 D-11-RE	42-75614		
		379th BG	AS	B-17 E	41-9100	Birmingham Blitzkrieg	6.44 – 6.45
			FM	?	?		
		384th BG	AS	B-17 F-60-DL	42-3441	The Spotted Cow (ex – Patches II)	7.44 – 5.45
			FM	P-47 D-10-RE	42-75154		
	94th CBW	351st BG	AS	B-17 G-5-VE	42-39914	The Black Bitch (ex – Lucky Strike)	? – 6.45
			FM	P-47 D-1-RE	42-7871		
		401st BG	AS	none			
			FM	P-47 D-2-RE	42-8226		
		457th BG	AS	none			
			FM	P-47 D-11-RE	42-75218		
2nd AD	2nd CBW	389th BG	AS	B-24 D-1-CO	41-23683	Green Dragon (ex – Jo Jo's Special Delivery)	12.43 – 7.44
			AS	B-24 J-55-CO	42-99972		7.44 – 5.45
			FM	P-47 D-5-RE	42-8532		
			FM	P-47 D-28-RA	42-28659	FAG	
		445th BG	AS	B-24 D-20-CO	41-24215	Lucky Gordon	1.44 – ?
			AS	B-24 H-xx-xx	unkn.		?
			FM	?			
		453rd BG	AS	B-24 D-1-CO	41-23738	Wham Bam	2.44 – 5.45
			FM	P-47 C-5-RE	41-6630		
	14th CBW	44th BG	AS	B-24 D-1-CO	41-23699	Lemon Drop	2.44 – 5.45
			AS	B-24 H-5-CF	41-29208	Shoo Shoo Baby	4.44 – 3.45
			FM	P-47 C-5-RE	41-6618		
			FM	P-47 D-1-RE	42-7865		
		392nd BG	AS	B-24 D-1-CO	41-23689	Minerva	1.44 – 10.44
			FM	P-47 D-11-RE	42-75434	Slugger	1.44 – 4.45
		491st BG	AS	B-24 D-90-CO	42-40722	The Little Gramper	6.44 – 8.44
			AS	B-24 J-150-CO	44-40165	Rage in Heaven	9.44 – 1.45
			AS	B-24 J-145-CO	44-40101	Tubarao	1.45 – 5.45
			FM	?			
		492nd BG	AS	B-24 D-95-CO	42-40743	Zebra	5.44 – 8.44
			FM	P-47 D-11-RE	42-75517	LuLu	7.44 – 8.44
			FM	P-47 D-1-RE	42-7xx7		
	20th CBW	93rd BG	AS	B-24 D-1-CO	41-23667	Ball Of Fire	11.43 – 9.44
			AS	B-24 D-165-CO	42-72869	Bear Down	7.44 – 5.45
			FM	P-47 D-x-Rx	42-xxxx		
		446th BG	AS	B-24 D-1-CO	41-23737	Fearless Freddie (ex – Eager Beaver)	2.44 – 10.44
			AS	B-24 H-1-FO	42-7654	Fearless Freddie II (ex – Pistol Packin Mamma)	9.44 – 1.45
			FM	P-47 C-5-RE	41-xxxx	The Old Man	
		448th BG	AS	B-24 D-5-CO	41-23809	You Cawn't Miss It (ex – Hellsadroppin' II)	2.44 – 6.44
			AS	B-24 D-20-CF	42-63981	The Striped Ape	6.44 – 2.45
			AS	B-24 H-15-CF	41-29489	The Striped Ape	2.45 – 5.45
			FM	P-47 C-5-RE	41-6380		
		489th BG	AS	B-24 H-1-FO	42-7552	Lil' Cookie	5.44 – 10.44
			FM	?			
2nd AD	96th CBW	458th BG	AS	B-24 D-30-CO	42-40127	First Sergeant	2.44 – 5.44
			AS	B-24 H-10-DT	41-28697	Spotted Ass Ape	5.44 – 3.45
			AS	B-24 J-95-CO	42-100366	Mizpah	3.45 – 5.45
			FM	P-47 D-25-RE	42-26560	Ginny	
		466th BG	AS	B-24 D-20-CO	41-24109	Ready & Willing	3.44 – 5.45
			?	B-24 H-20-CF	42-50288	Dumbo	1.45 – 5.45
			FM	P-47 D-11-RE	42-75517	Sally	8.44 – ?
		467th BG	AS	B-24 D-53-CO	42-40370	Pete, The POM Inspector (ex – Heaven Can Wait)	3.44 – 10.44
			AS	B-24 H-15-CF	41-29393	Pete, The POM Inspector 2nd (ex – Shoo-Shoo Baby)	10.44 – 5.45
			?	B-24 J-50-CO	42-73512		
			FM	P-47 D-23-RA	42-27790	Little Pete	
			FM	P-47 D-25-RE	42-26393	Little Pete 2	
		94th BG	AS	none			
			FM	?			
		447th BG	AS	none			
			FM	?			
	4th CBW	486th BG	AS	B-17 F-90-BO	42-30145	Green Hornet	2.44 – 5.45
			FM	P-47 D-6-RE	42-74680		
		487th BG	AS	none			
			FM	?			
3rd AD	13th CBW	95th BG	AS	none			
			FM	?			
		100th BG	AS	none			
			AS	P-47 D-2-RE	42-8372		
			FM	P-47 D-22-RE	42-25745		
		390th BG	AS	none			
			FM	?			
	45th CBW	96th BG	AS	none			
			FM	?			
		388th BG	AS	none			
			FM	?			
		452nd BG	AS	none			
			FM	?			
	93rd CBW	34th BG	AS	none			
			FM	P-51	unkn.		
			FM	P-47	unkn.		
		385th BG	AS	none			
			FM	?			
		490th BG	AS	none			
			FM	?			
		493rd BG	AS	none			
			FM	?			

Assembly Ships

The first air combat of WWII between RAF bombers and Luftwaffe fighters took place on the 18th December 1939. When twenty-four Wellingtons of Nos. 9, 37, and 149 Squadrons took off on an armed reconnaissance sortie over the Helgoland Bay (two of them returned early due to technical problems). It was a bright, sunny day, and the sky was clear of clouds, but no targets were visible, so the Wellingtons headed for home with their bomb load still on board. However, the formation was spotted by the German radar system, and sixteen Bf 110s and thirty-four Bf 109s were sent to intercept. The fighters used whatever tactics they wanted towards the slow bombers, attacking them from every direction, so they could choose the best range at which to open fire. The combat resulted in twelve bombers being shot down, plus three badly damaged Wellingtons that eventually got back to base. From this incident, the RAF learned a vital lesson: as long as the slow bombers could not have fighter protection, or the attack could not be delivered through cloud cover, the only way to survive was to operate at night. For many reasons, such a proposal was a very complicated endeavor. At the time, the technology did not exist to drop bombs accurately on a specific target area, and the RAF had thus undertaken not to attack targets at night that might endanger civilian lives. Both of these factors therefore dictated strategic rather than carpet bombing. The RAF's strategic bomber offensive began following Germany's attack on Rotterdam when, on the 15th May 1940, the new Prime Minister, Winston Churchill, lifted the ban on not provoking the Germans to counter-attacks. That very night, ninety-nine RAF bombers delivered an attack on railway and oil targets in the Ruhr Valley.

The calm before the storm... A row of Liberators of the 466th BG parked on the hard standing.

Preparation. Loading bombs and ammunition for Brownings. Fortresses of the 91st BG being bombed up.

At this stage of the war night bombing operations had one thing in common: they were, to put it mildly, inaccurate. Prime Minister Churchill's scientific adviser, Professor Lindemann, asked Mr. D. Butt of the War Cabinet Secretariat to conduct an independent inquiry into the effectiveness of night bombing. The results were extremely disappointing, as even in good weather conditions during a bright summer night, only one in five bombs landed within nine kilometers of the target! During the biggest bombing raid over Germany, on 7th/8th November 1941, the RAF lost 37 aircraft out of the 392 sent, but the target remained untouched. During the first eighteen months of night bombing raids from May 1940, bomber crews had acted off their initiative. It was their decision at what altitude to reach enemy territory and which route to take back home. To the crew, the bomber's safe return was the priority; after all, they were the ones to survive. However, the growing number of losses in the last four months of 1942, a direct result of the Himmelbett system's extreme success, forced the British to change their tactics. The way to lessen the losses was to send bombers in a concentrated mass. A single Himmelbett station could guide one nightfighter to intercept one bomber, thus enabling roughly about six interceptions per hour. When the bombers arrived one by one over a long period of time, they could easily be intercepted and destroyed. Thus, the risk of collision was only 0.5 percent, while the probability of being shot down was 3-4 percent, a fact that made the planners' choice clear. The word 'concentration' in this context meant a flight of aircraft that would pass over a target with ten bombers per hour. Each group of ten bombers created a box that was eight kilometers wide, three and a half high, and five kilometers long, and this gave no chance of producing combined firepower to protect the formation, as the aircraft were too spaced out. During the first RAF 'thousand bomber raids' on Cologne on the 30th April – 1st May 1942, the bomber stream was set to deliver eleven aircraft over the target every ten minutes.

In late 1942, the United States Army Air Force (USAAF) joined the battle over Germany. To the surprise and irritation of the British, the Americans insisted on daylight raids over the Reich and occupied territories. From business, journalistic, or maybe even political sources, the Americans knew about

Strong and ready. 457th BG B-17s parked at Burtonwood.

Warming up the engines. 487th BG B-24s lined up for take-off at Lavenham.

the poor raid effectiveness of the RAF. The American commanders believed that only daylight attacks could give the desired accuracy. But until the introduction of long-range fighters, the bombers' best defence would be their formation and the concentrated firepower this offered. Initially, during the battle over Europe, the USAAF was equipped with two types of strategic bombers: the B-17E Flying Fortress and B-24D Liberator, which were later replaced with the newer B-17F and G and B-24H and J. These machines were designed to be operated by both mechanics and flight crew with only very limited training. Not without good reason did the American planners think that good armour, heavy calibre 0.5in machine-guns, and a high degree of mutual fire support would reduce the danger of fighter attacks, while the efficiency of flak would be lessened due to the high altitudes at which these machines would operate. The first small-scale raid delivered by the US Eighth Air Force took place on 17th August 1942, when twelve B-17s delivered an attack on a shipyard near Rouen, France. The short distance to the target and protection offered by Spitfires avoided high losses in this instance. However, the first major attack of 108 bombers that took place on 7th October 1942 met with resistance from JG 2 and JG 26. The USAAF lost four aircraft, while the Luftwaffe lost two. This combat determined the shape of those that would follow in the coming two and half years, and would ultimately cost the lives of thousands of pilots.

The Eighth Air Force attacked, on the 27th January 1943, the naval shipyard at Wilhelmshaven, and the naval munitions depot at nearby Mariensiel. The bombing zone was obscured by clouds, and only 55 of the 91 bombers reached the target, but the raid was considered a success. The Luftwaffe pilots shot down three American aircraft but lost seven of their own in the process. The preceding visit by ninety-three B-17s and B-24s over Germany on the 26th January 1943 had cost the USAAF seven aircraft, including one that was shot down by anti-aircraft artillery. The third raid on the shipyard in Vegesack took place on 18th March 1943 when ninety-seven USAAF bombers were attacked by fifty Luftwaffe

Readiness. 491st BG lined up on the perimeter track at Metfield before a mission.

Taxiing and start: B-17s of the 91st BG (above) and aircraft of the 96th BG (below and bottom).

Up in the air! A low flight of Liberators of the 491st BG soon after a take-off.

Forming a box. Rendezvous with an assembly ship. A machine of the 458th BG. The picture was taken from the waist window of First Sergeant, the Group's first assembly aircraft – see pages 99-100.

Forming 'the box' is finished. The assembly ship leaves a formation and returns to its base. Aircraft of the 458th BG across the English Channel.

fighters, but these achieved only two victories and the raid was considered a great success. The result of this operation convinced the American High Command that the mass defensive fire offered by the bombers' 0.5in machine-guns was a lethal obstacle for enemy fighters. However, it would not be long before the Luftwaffe would send more and more Messerschmitt and Focke-Wulf fighters to counter the USAAF bomber groups. Up to this point the aircraft flew in eighteen-aircraft boxes at approximately two and a half kilometre intervals and the entire Combat Wing stretched over 5 kilometres. However, since the third bombing raid the layout looked different with three bomb groups positioned one above the other, the lead box in the middle and the lower one just behind the other two. Squeezed up in a smaller space, the bomb group, in a 1,800-metre wide, 600 metre high, and 900 metre long box, was like a fortress full of machine-guns. There were eleven-kilometre intervals between each combat wing. The first operation in this new formation was carried out on 17th April 1943 against the Focke-Wulf facility near Vagesack. The aircraft gathering over England were picked-up by the German radar system, and two groups of JG 1 engaged the bombers before they reached the target. During the ensuing battle, the US Eighth Air Force suffered its most serious loss with fifteen bombers shot down by enemy fighters, a single aircraft by flak, and another forty-eight were damaged. The operation did not give any answer whether the new formation was effective or not but what had been proved was that a formation of 54 aircraft was too big to be commanded effectively. In the first stage of operation fighters were the real danger to the bombers. Bomber operations during 1943 showed that 48 out of the first 100 B-17s and B-24s shot down were lost when they were flown in a formation, while the rest were lost after they left the formation due to damage or other reasons. However, of the 48 shot down within the formation, only 26 were shot down by fighters instead of 46 of the 52 that had left the formation. This highlighted that raids delivered in formations resulted in fewer losses, and further analysis indicated that bomb release on the commander's signal created a kind of

'Little friends' – long-range escort fighters join the formation. Mustangs of the 352nd FG beside Liberators of the 458th BG.

En route. Target: Germany. A bomber formation of the 458th BG with Mustangs as company.

The 381st BG (top and above) and the 91st BG (below, right).

'carpet' of explosions on the target. However, even during these so-called 'precision' daylight raids 50% Circular Error was about 430 metres (Circular Error = the radius of a circle, with the centre at a desired mean point of impact, which contains half the bombs independently aimed to hit the desired mean point of impact) and in bad weather this went up to as high as 1,100 metres! During the summer of 1943, the RAF achieved a result of 650 metres, thanks mainly to their use of the Oboe electronic system. A bomb raid on Emden on 27th September 1943 was the next stage of the US Eighth Air Force's bombing campaign, as it was at this stage that aircraft with radar were introduced when the target was obscured by clouds. It was also the first bombing raid with fighter cover all the way along the bombers' route to and from the target – two hundred and fifty P-47s shot down twenty German fighters. All these changes did not affect the formation, the so-called 'Combat Box'. This particular formation was developed by General Curtis LeMay and was based on his experience as a US Eighth Air Force strategic bomber group commander. The US Eighth Air Force Bomb Groups had used various formation schemes with varying degrees of success beginning in 1942, but the Combat Box formation had eventually become standard for all US Eighth Air Force group formations. The Combat Box was accepted as the best arrangement of aircraft to maximise firepower from all guns, while providing a bombing pattern with the maximum effect on the target.

The Combat Box formation was made up of a number of basic airplane layouts. From the smallest to the largest, these formations were:
- Element Formation: 3 aircraft
- Squadron Formation: four elements – 12 aircraft
- Group Formation: three squadrons – 36 aircraft
- Wing Formation: three groups – 108 aircraft

During the approach, each element and squadron would come in formations one after the other over the initial point. After the bomb release, aircraft dropped to approximately 700 metres to gain some speed and mislead the anti-aircraft crews. The last stage was to create a V-formation at the formatting point. At the end of 1944 and into early 1945, when every mission was supported by fighters, mutual fire support lost its significance and boxes therefore consisted of thirty-six aircraft. However, a Lead, High and Low Squadron arrangement remained unchanged until the end of the war. With the growing number of aircraft sent over the Third Reich, the time needed for assembling a mission lengthened. To put every bomber into Elements, Squadrons and Groups in a set time took nothing less than blood, sweat and tears. The credit for the success goes to headquarter and group

Element Formation

An Element of three aircraft was the basic unit in all formations. The element lead was responsible for maintaining his element's position relative to the squadron lead at all times. One aircraft flew off his port (left) wing and one off his starboard (right). Those flying the left and right wing positions were responsible for staying in 'tight formation' with the element lead at all times, but on the bombing run to the target in particular. The element wing positions tried to maintain their positions about the same altitude, one wing length horizontally from and one wing length behind the element lead.

This basic Element Formation was really the most tedious and perhaps dangerous formation to fly because of the proximity of each aircraft and the reliance on the 'other guy' to do his job reasonably well. Usually, the pilot/co-pilot took turns, perhaps fifteen minutes or so at a time, maintaining their plane's position regarding the element lead. In a tight formation, the vertical and horizontal distances between each plane of the element were based on a few inconsistent factors. Bombers should have been close enough to have their neighbours' support, though far enough away in case of a shell or rocket explosion that would therefore destroy only one aircraft. The optimum distance between wingtips was about seventy metres, and the range of the Flak 36 88 mm shell was about 30 metres.

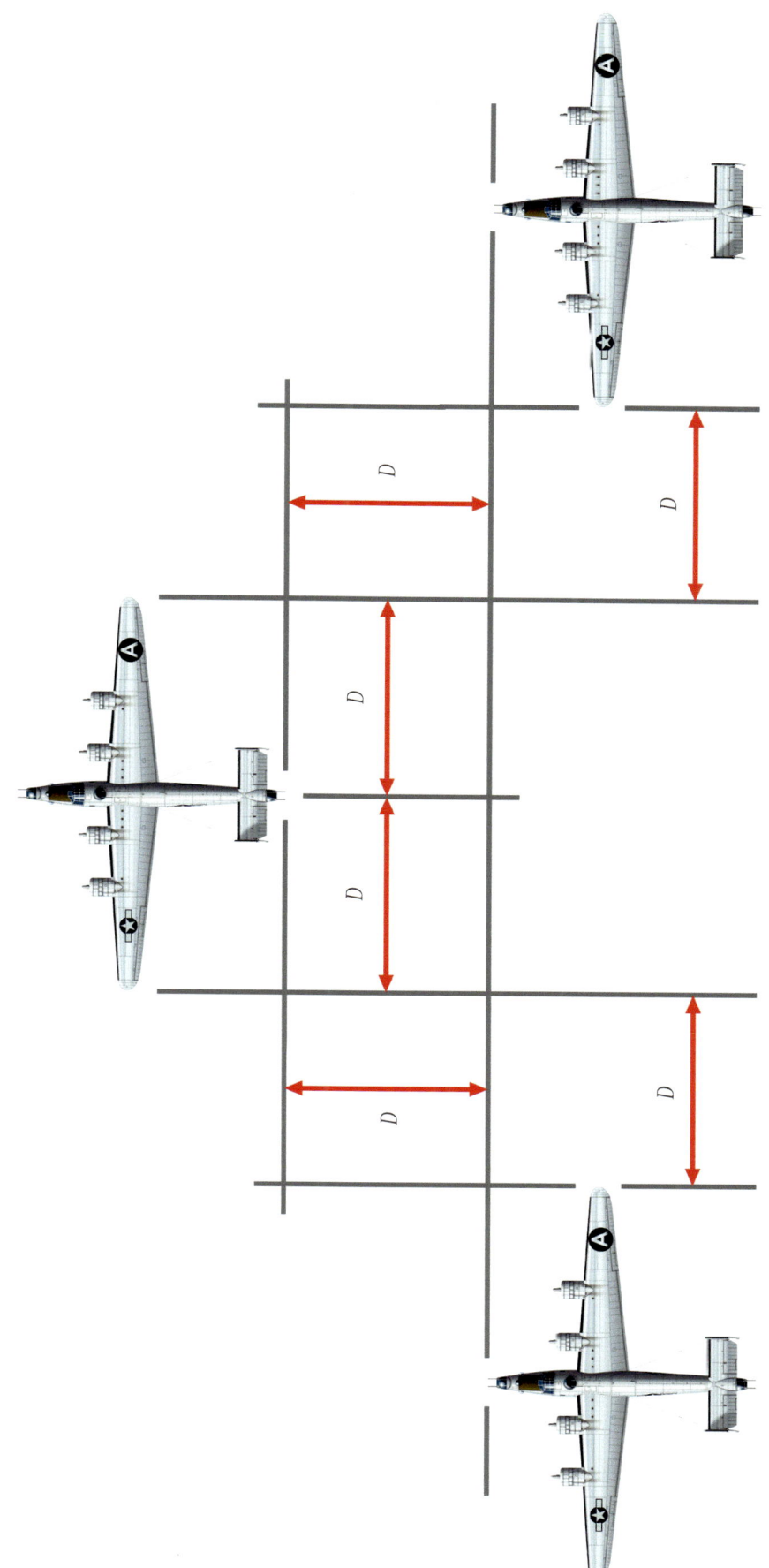

Squadron Formation

Squadron Formation

There were several squadron formations tried and used with varying degrees of success during the US Eighth Air Force's time in combat. The Squadron Box Formation was made up of four element formations, each like the one described above. The four elements of the squadron formation were arranged as follows:

- The Lead Element became the Squadron lead, with the other three Elements flying positions all oriented on his lead position. The High Element flew above, to the right and behind the Squadron Lead.
- The Low Element flew below, to the left and behind the lead, the Squadron Lead.
- The Low Low Element flew directly below and behind the Squadron Lead.

In some historic records, the positions flown by the pilots in the formation are indicated in the text. It should be noted, though, that there is no standardization in the records of the abbreviated formation position names.

Group Formation

A three-squadron formation formed a Group Formation. The basic squadron formation described above became one of the three-squadron formations that comprised the Group Formation. The Group Formation was identified with that group's insignia, such as the triangle (1st Air Division), circle (2nd Air Division) or square (3rd Air Division) with a capital letter assigned to each Group, painted on the upper starboard wing and both vertical tail surfaces.

- *The Lead Squadron formation of twelve planes was in front.*
- *The High Squadron formation flew above, behind and to the right of the lead.*
- *The Low Squadron formation flew below, behind and to the left of the lead.*

Distances between the squadron formations were measured in hundreds of metres.

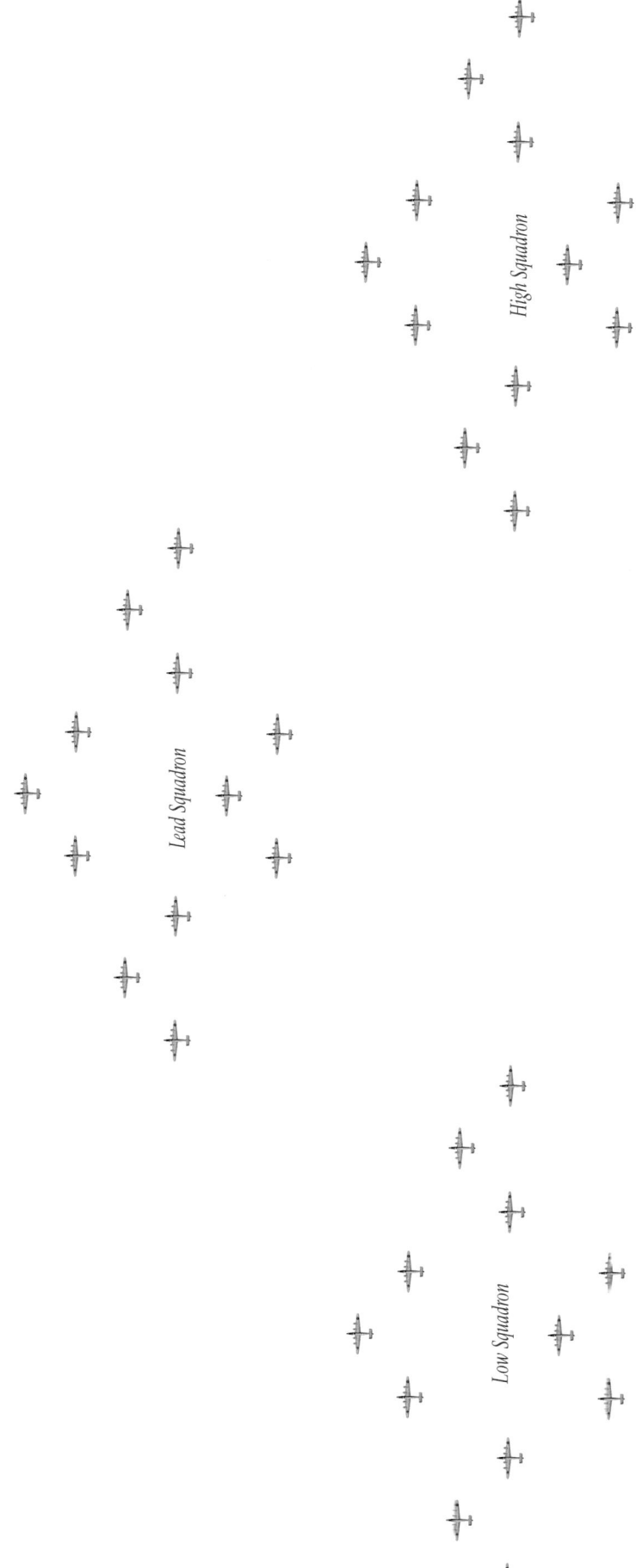

Wing Formation

The positioning relationship of the groups that comprised the wing continued the lead, high and low formation concept. That is to say that the terms lead, high and low also referred to the positioning of the individual group formations in relation to each other in the Wing formation. Again there was a Group Lead, Group High, and Group Low arrangement in the Wing Formation.

- *The Lead Bomb Group formation of thirty-six planes was the front of the Wing.*
- *The High Bomb Group formation flew above, behind and to the right of the lead.*
- *The Low Bomb Group formation flew below, behind and to the left of the lead.*

Distances between the group formations were measured in a few thousands of metres. However, it must be said that the prescribed and actual flying distances between all the formations at any time varied due to weather, combat conditions and flying skills.

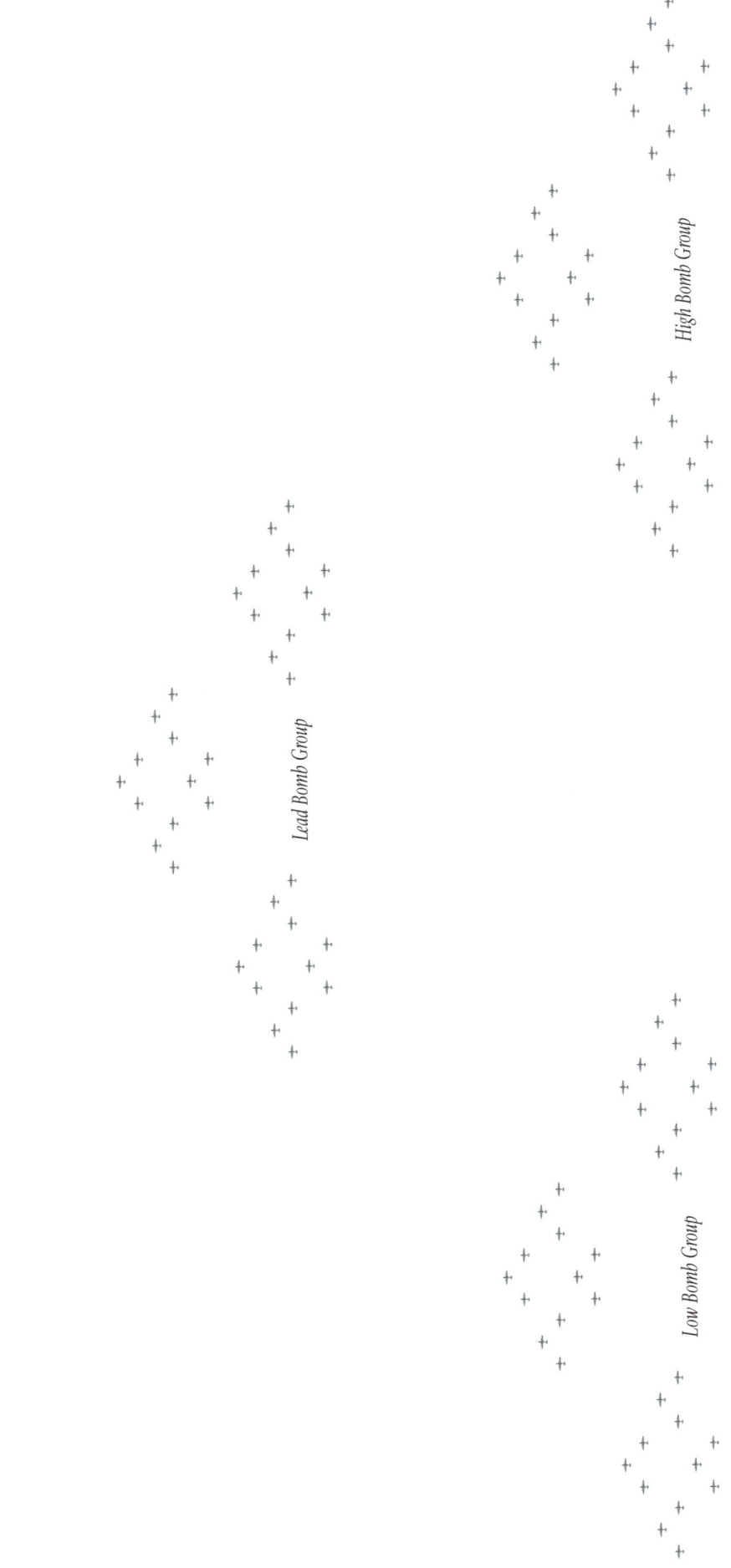

Modified Box Formation

Beginning in late February 1945, the well-established and standard Box Formation used by the groups was modified. Instead of four three-aircraft elements comprising a Squadron Formation as described above, that Squadron Formation was changed to three elements of four aircraft each. The three aircraft that previously had formed the Low Low Element in the old Squadron Formation were used to fill the three slot positions of the Lead, High and Low elements of the new Squadron Formation. The slot position was directly behind, but lower than the Element lead. All three squadrons of the Group Formation flew in this new revised formation. There were no changes in the relationship of the squadrons in the group formation. Thus, a squadron still flew 12 aircraft, but in three elements of four aircraft. There is no definitive history as to why this change took place, but it probably involved a decision about providing a better bomb impact pattern.

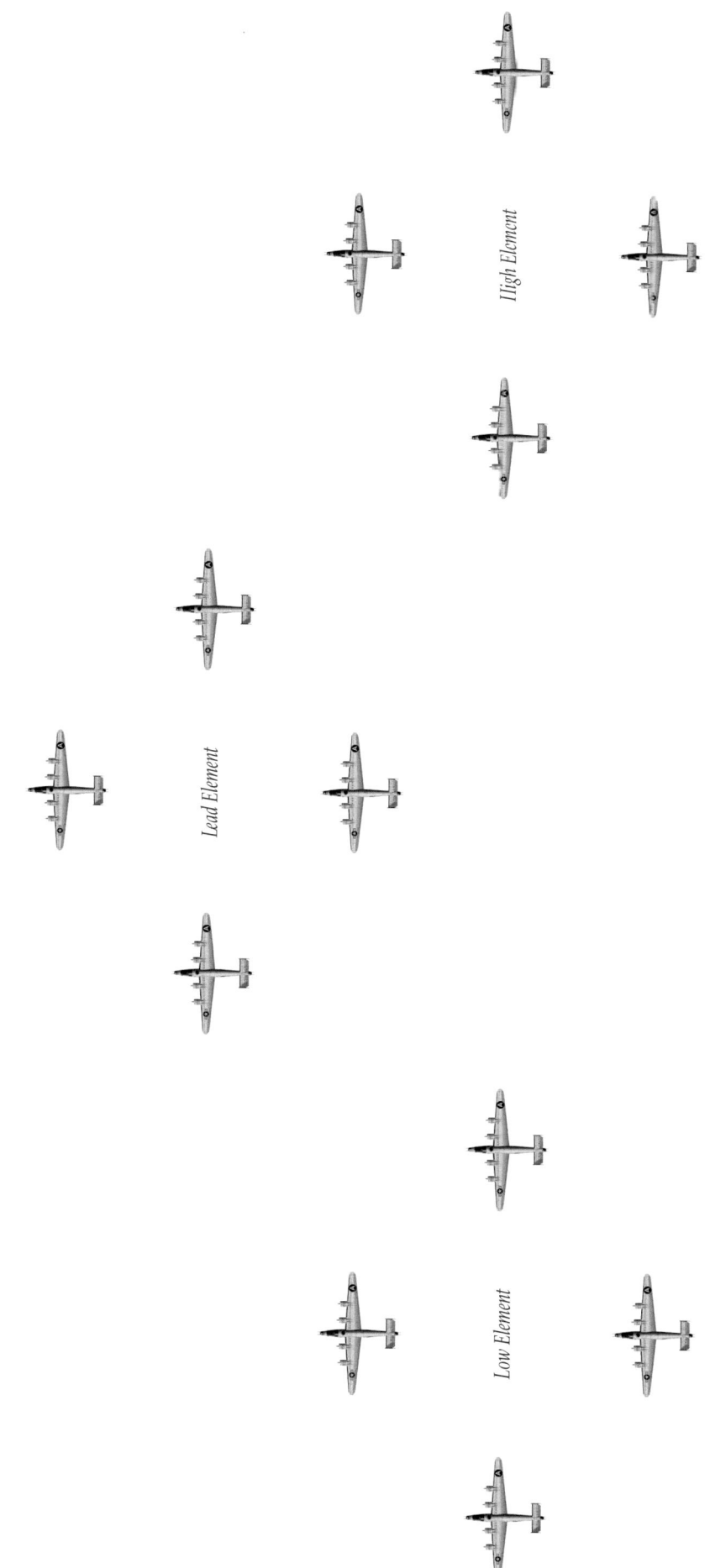

The sight of B-17s in formation became a symbol of USAAF power. 384th BG (above), 100th BG (left), B-17s formations seen from below (bottom).

Over the target area one could always expect heavy flak. A pathfinder leader ship of the 93rd BG with radome lowered is targeting he drop point.

commanders and, according to one of the American pilots, "the assembly process could, and did, consume two to three hours. Under ideal conditions (I never saw that in England), it could be just one hour." Many veterans say that forming a combat box was a big challenge, just try to imagine a combat wing of sixty aircraft taking off every 30 seconds and it would still take half an hour for the last aircraft to join the formation. As each box was formed, it would head for the coast to get into an assigned position within the bomber stream. This is how Capt. Robert Copp, pilot of a B-24D of the 392nd Bomb Group, remembers the assembly process over England:

"On that Saturday morning, April 29th, our taxi time was 7:25 a.m., take-off was at 7:30 and assembly was accomplished at 9:20. That's almost two hours and a good deal of the mission right there. It all depends on the weather and altitude. They may have said, "Assembly at 10,000ft" Well, you go up to that height and you may still be in the Scud [cloud]. You might have to go up a little higher to 12,000ft or more. What used to make us madder than hell was to get up there, get all assembled out over the channel and then, have them scrub the mission for some reason. It was no picnic to be up there for two or more hours with your buddies flying all over the sky. There was some resemblance to what it was suppose to be, but it was a tricky operation.

If you ever saw the take-off pattern, you'd be amazed. Flares are shooting off all over the morning sky, and after I take-off, all the rest of the planes in our group follow us up through the fog. We'd fly back and forth until you pick up all your people and get them into formation. Then our box would have to be at a certain 'buncher' at a certain time. On the 29th, we were to fly high right to the 44th Bomb Group, so finding them was our next job. You look all around and say, "Geez, we're supposed to be over here now." So the 392nd would wheel around and pick up the 44th. They in turn would fall behind the 398th or the 492nd Bomb Group and form the 14th Combat Wing; then we'd all follow the 2nd Air Division which was only part of the Eight Air Force bomber stream.

Believe me, there were times when everything didn't go quite as planned. On one occasion, I actually went all the way to Kiel by myself. I couldn't find anyone from my group. I thought to myself: "Boy, this is ridiculous! What the hell are we doing way out here all alone?" Luckily, no fighters picked us up and I came in with a bunch of B-17's. I came within 50 feet of them with all our guys waving and shooting flares and what not...just to tell them: "Hey, we're your buddies!" You're not supposed to break radio silence and even if we had, they wouldn't have known for sure if we were the enemy! We had heard, they had some of our airplanes and were attacking us, right in our own formations. All those B-17's could do was to judge us by our actions. It was a funny feeling to have all those guns pointing at us. I don't think they trusted us until we went in at I.P. and dropped bombs with them".

Each aircraft (a small, two-centimetre line represents a B-17 Flying Fortress seen from the distance of four kilometres) made it difficult to find your place in a formation. To help find comrades from a formation, assembly ships were introduced. These were planes painted in strange, distinctive colours, and stripped of armament and part of their equipment to reduce overall weight and thus help the engines to run smoothly for many hours. An assembly ship was the first to take-off, and it would then circle over the rendezvous point and wait for the other aircraft to arrive. Bombers, climbing away at 100 metres per minute, would gather at 2,300 to 3,000 metres, then proceed to another assembly area and then head for the target. To help find a group and assigned position, assembly ships fired off flares of the group's

After locating the target, the leading aircraft releases smoke markers. Above: Liberators of the 467th BG in action.

Bombs away! Liberators of the 446th BG (above) and the 467th BG (below) release their bombs.

In units with Flying Fortresses, a mission over the target was similar to that of the units with Liberators. First, Pathfinders locate the target. Above: two "Mickey" machines of the 96th BG.

colours. What should be remembered is that radio silence was maintained when forming groups over England. In all the chaos of the assembly process (sometimes bases were located 5 minutes flight away from each other) the pilots would attach to other combat boxes. When all the aircraft had found their assigned positions, the assembly ships' impressive, but useful, mission was finished. All assembly ships were flown by pilots not assigned to combat missions at that time. What is interesting is that assembly ships were used mostly in the Liberator bombing groups, but rarely by Flying Fortress units. The most significant users of such aircraft were the 303rd, 370th and 384th BG. However, the group commanders found that this assembly process had little advantage over group leaders firing flares, and they disliked the idea of using precious fuel over the British Isles. No matter how ordinary the assembly ships' missions were, they played a significant role in helping combat aircraft pilots to create a formation before a raid. In 1944, the so-called Buncher radio beacons were introduced and each base had its own, broadcasting at specific frequencies. The combat formations were put together by adjusting their position to an assigned radio signal. However, this was only a supplement to already-existing ways of assembling formations, so assembly ships were still used until the end of the war. Most of the assembly aircraft were war-weary B-24Ds, Hs, and a few B-17s. It is worth making mention of Dr. A. Price's description of the assembly process of the 348th BG before their raid over Berlin on 18th March 1945.

"The first aircraft took off at 7.00 hours and the last one at 8.16 hours. At 8.37 hours the 384th BG reached the Wing Assembly Point over March, where other groups arrived in two minute intervals. Then, at 8.55 hours the groups' bombers attached to the other groups and divisions over Cromer (Divisional Assembly Point) where they headed to France. To reach each route marker at the exact time B-17 groups would not fly straight but make some turns. Thanks to cutting short or extending such dog-leg turn overs it was possible to control the time without reducing the airspeed. Altering the speed would have caused the formation to lose cohesion. The importance of precise planning was best seen in the formation of 1221 B-17s and B-24s stretched along 330 kilometres during their raid over Berlin on 18th March 1945."

The role of war-weary fighters assigned to each Group – especially P-47s – was much different. These were so-called police aircraft, or formation monitors. Pilots would call them 'Dogs' or 'Cops'. Their task was to control aircraft so that they could find their assigned position, and similar to shepherd dogs, they would gee dawdling bombers up, and help them to join their 'flock'. Remembering that any radio contact was strictly forbidden, signals like 'follow me' were very useful during an assembly. Regardless of the hard work of the assembly aircraft and 'dogs', the great number of mid-air collisions show that the task of assembling the bombers before a mission was extremely difficult to perform, though.

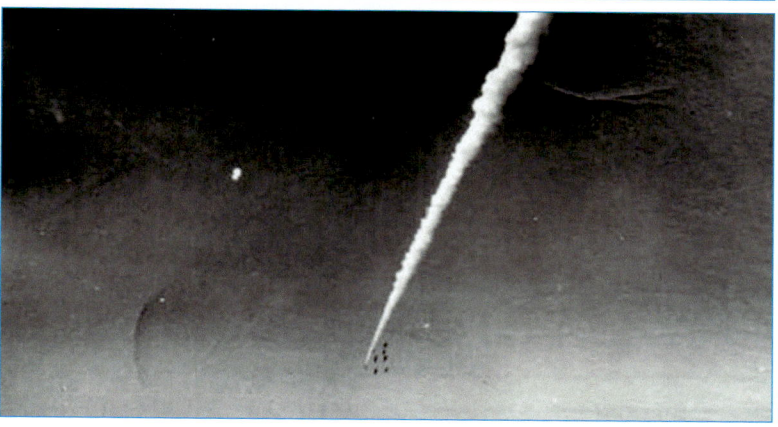

The lead plane releases smoke markers to mark the aiming points for the raids. Above and below: the 100th BG in action.

Showtime! Flying Fortresses of the 447th BG (above) and bombers of the 91st BG (below) in action.

Over the target – a beautiful shot of a Fortress over the Berlin-Tempelhof area.

Mission accomplished! B-17s of the 398th BG close their bomb bay doors.

The return. Aircraft of the 381st BG over English fields.

Home Sweet Home. Bird's eye view of Horsham St. Faith, base of the 458th BG.

The last dangerous stage of the mission, landing. First aid unit. An ambulance and a fire fighter unit await the safe return of an aircraft.

Only a few hundred meters... B-24D s/n 41-23809 Hellsadroppin' II of the 93rd BG landing at Hardwick. This Liberator was later transferred to the 448th BG to become the group's assembly ship, You Cawn't Miss It – see pages 103–105.

Another mission accomplished. The aircraft is the caring mechanics' hands. B-24D, s/n 42-40743 of the 389th BG undergoing engine maintenance on its hardstanding at Hethel. The plane was eventually transferred to the 492nd BG and became the group's assembly ship named Zebra – see pages 75–77.

Before they became assembly ships: B-24J s/n 44-40165 Rage In Heaven of the 491st BG – later to become the group's second assembly aircraft (above); B-24D s/n 41-24109 Ready & Willing of the 93rd BG – later to become an assembly aircraft of the 466th BG (below left); B-24H s/n 41-29393 Shoo-Shoo Baby of the 467th BG – later to become 'Pete The P.O.M. Inspector 2nd', an assembly aircraft of its group (below right).

B-24D s/n 42-40722 The Little Gramper of the 389th BG – later to become the first assembly aircraft of the 491st BG (above left); B-24J s/n 44-40101 Tubarão of the 491st BG – later to become the group's third assembly aircraft (above right); B-24J s/n 42-100366 Mizpah of the 458th BG (below left); B-24D s/n 41-21738 Wham Bam of the 93rd BG – later to become an assembly aircraft of the 453rd BG (below right).

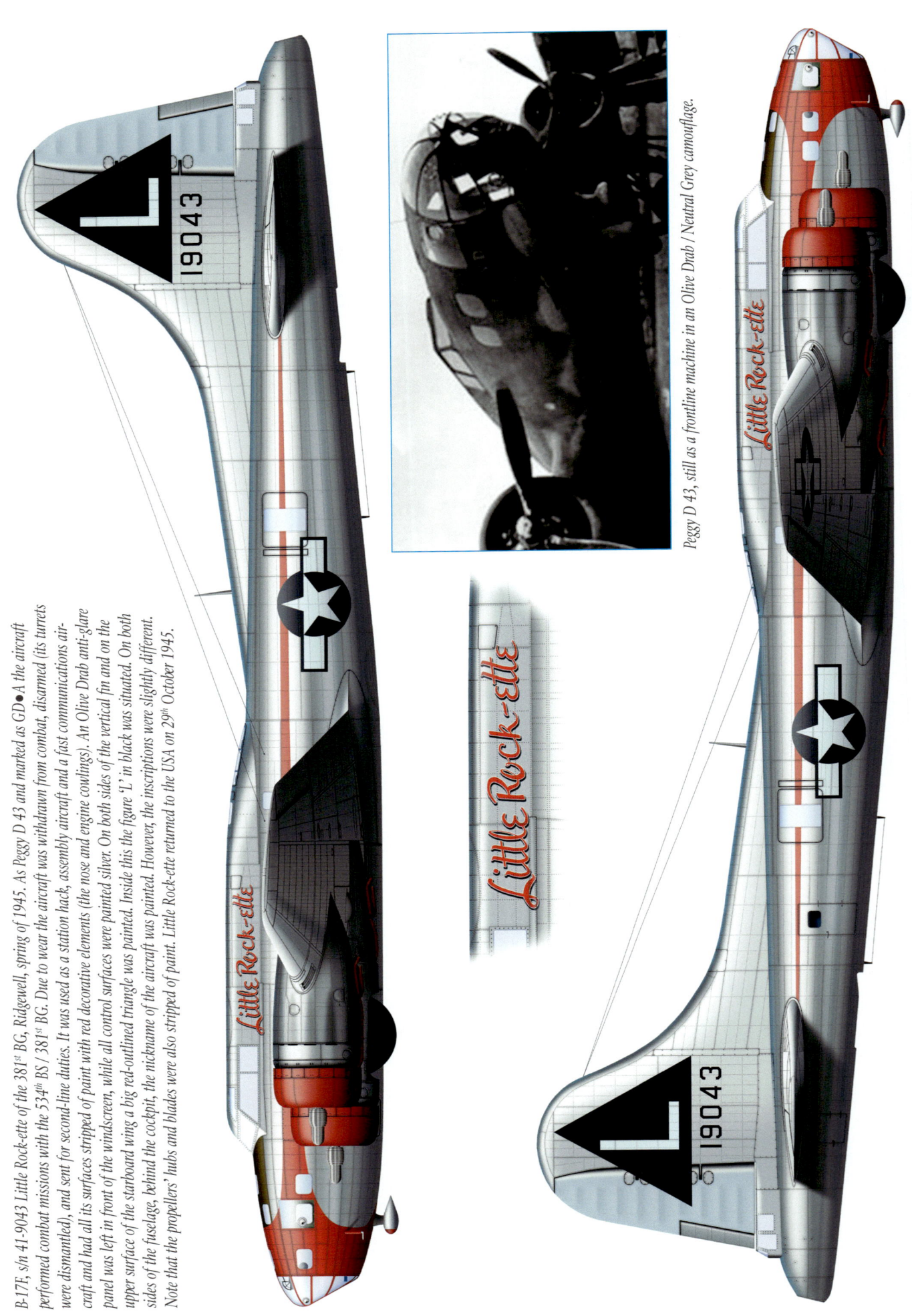

Peggy D 43, still as a frontline machine in an Olive Drab / Neutral Grey camouflage.

B-17F, s/n 41-9043 Little Rock-ette of the 381st BG, Ridgewell, spring of 1945. As Peggy D 43 and marked as GD●A the aircraft performed combat missions with the 534th BS / 381st BG. Due to wear the aircraft was withdrawn from combat, disarmed (its turrets were dismantled), and sent for second-line duties. It was used as a station hack, assembly aircraft and a fast communications aircraft and had all its surfaces stripped of paint with red decorative elements (the nose and engine cowlings). An Olive Drab anti-glare panel was left in front of the windscreen, while all control surfaces were painted silver. On both sides of the vertical fin and on the upper surface of the starboard wing a big red-outlined triangle was painted. Inside this the figure 'L' in black was situated. On both sides of the fuselage, behind the cockpit, the nickname of the aircraft was painted. However, the inscriptions were slightly different. Little Rock-ette returned to the USA on 29th October 1945. Note that the propellers' hubs and blades were also stripped of paint.

B-17E s/n 41-9043 Little Rock-ette. An excerpt from the 448th SubDepot Diary when the ship was modified. Entry is from February 1944 by subdepot commander, Major Raymond Jolicoeur: "Another never to be forgotten ship was the target ship stationed at our field – the B-17E – 41-9043 (534th GD*A-1 LITTLE ROCK-ETTE, after formerly being PEGGY D originally with 97th BG). It was desired to make an assembly and weather ship out of it; so the work of modifying it was started by the Depot Fabric Shop. All they had to do was remove all the paints from the ship and paint fancy red stripes here and there on it. They did an impressive job though and broke the ice for other depts who had to:

1. Manufacture and install 12 floodlights to illuminate the ship while in flight;
2. Change engines and props;
3. Put a floor in the bomb bay;
4. Relocate oxygen system under floor in bomb bay;
5. Install two additional seats behind pilot and co-pilot's seats;
6. Install 56" wheels and accompanying equipment."

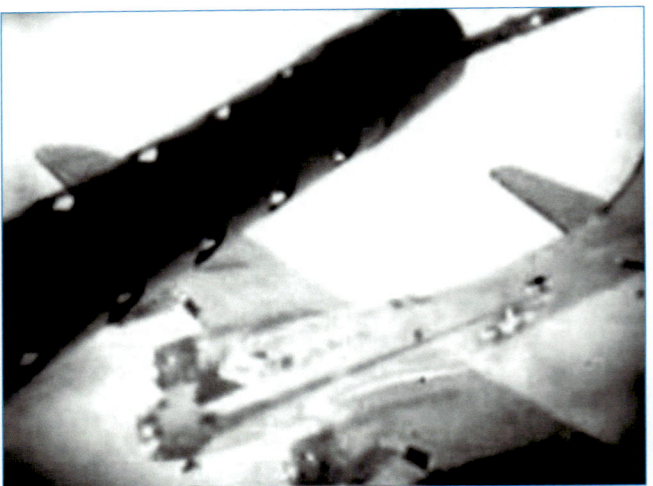

Colonel Hall indeed named the plane after his home (Little Rock, state of Arkansas). Some pilots who flew 'Little Rock-ette' said, it was a great plane to fly with the reduced weight and other modifications.
The opposite page, top: *41-9043 as 'Pegy D-43' had participated in the first 'heavy' mission of the Mighty Eighth at Rouen on the 17th August 1942. Here seen in her days of glory.*
The opposite page, middle: *two frames with 'Little Rock-ette' taken from amateur movie recorded during 381st box assembly.*
The opposite page, bottom: *a beautiful shot of the 'Little Rock-ette' parked at Ridgewell.*
Below: *Brig Gen Williams converses with Gen Kepner, Col Gross and other officer at Ridgewell airfield. Note 'Little Rock-ette' in the background.*

Another picture of Little Rock-ette. This time the starboard side of the nose.

*P-47 D-10-RE s/n 42-75151 MX*L, 1st Combat Bombardment Wing's formation monitor. Initially, with the 78th Fighter Group (82nd FS) and later transferred to 1st CBW Headquarter Flight. Here you see the plane in the first stage of the markings during its career with 1st CBW, when retained all markings of the previous operator.*

P-47 D-10-RE s/n 42-75151 MX*L, here in the second stage of the markings during it's service with 1st CBW, when engine cowling is rapainted with Olive Drab and fin, horizontal stabilizers and wing tips are red like Fortresses of the 91st BG.

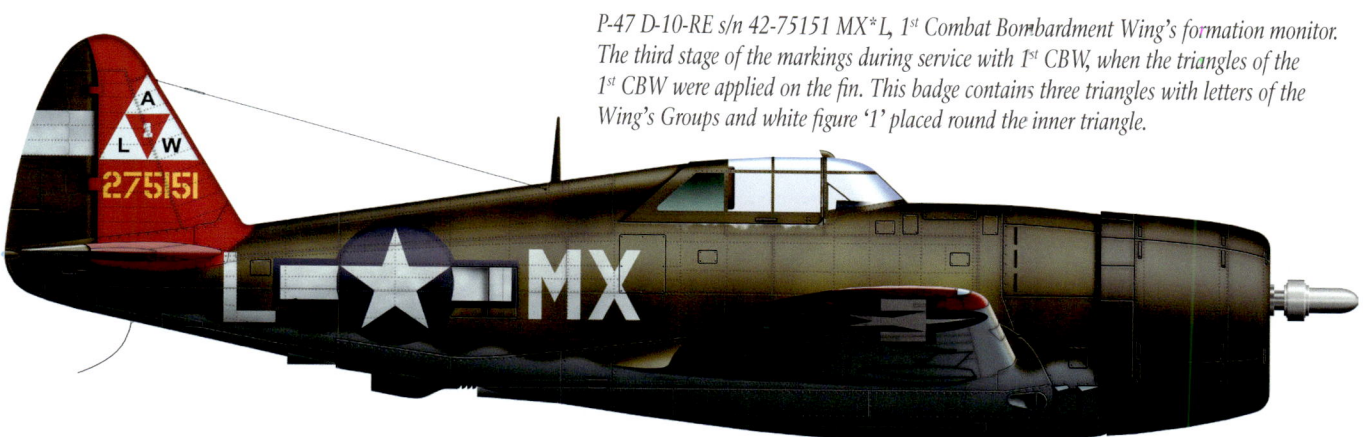

P-47 D-10-RE s/n 42-75151 MX*L, 1st Combat Bombardment Wing's formation monitor. The third stage of the markings during service with 1st CBW, when the triangles of the 1st CBW were applied on the fin. This badge contains three triangles with letters of the Wing's Groups and white figure '1' placed round the inner triangle.

P-47 D-10-RE s/n 42-75151 MX*L, 91st Bomb Group's formation monitor. The fourth stage of the markings during service with 1st CBW, after being transferred directly to the 91st BG. The triangle of the 1st CBW was repainted with a yellow triangle and 91st BG's badge within.

P-47D-15-RE s/n 42-75621, formation monitor of the 305th BG, Chelveston, 1945. The whole aircraft is natural dural colour. On the vertical tail fin there is a Triangle/G situated on a green horizontal line. Note that the aircraft lacks machine-guns, gunsight, and armoured glass panel. However, the machine was fitted with a D/F loop.

P-47 D-5-RE s/n 42-8442, the formation monitor of the 381st Bomb Group.

Thurleigh control tower, 1945. Note Thunderbolt s/n 42-8391 on the left.

P-47 D-2-RE s/n 42-8391, assigned as formation monitor to the 40th Combat Bombardment Wing's Headquarter Flight at Sta.111 / Thurleigh.

Hairless Joe after a belly landing at Lyons Farm, Bulcamp on 3rd February 1944.

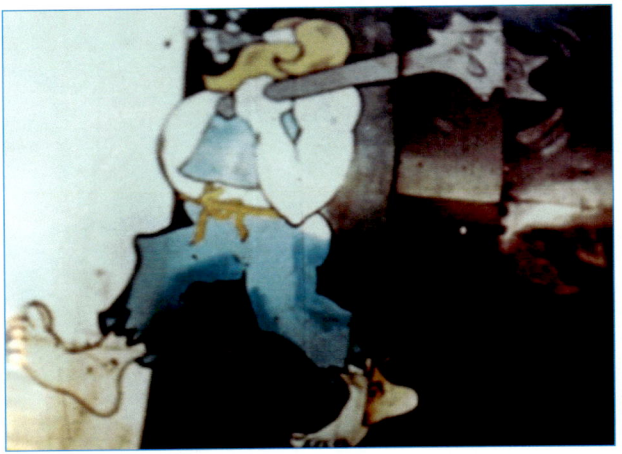

Hairless Joe motif on the engine cowling.

P-47D-15-RE s/n 42-7938 at the time when it was transferred as the formation monitor to the 306th BG at Thurleigh. The previous user of this Thunderbolt was the 62nd FS / 56th FG, where, until half way through January 1944 it was the personal machine of Maj. David Schilling, Deputy CO of the 56th FG. The machine ended its fighter career with 56th FG on 3rd February 1944, when its pilot, Lt John Fields, carried out a forced landing at Lyons Farm, Bulcamp after exhausting his fuel to-wards the end of a mission. After renovation, the aircraft was given a war-weary status, and allocated to second-line duties. Additionally, the aircraft's armament and gunsight were removed. The foundation's 'Hewlett – Woodmere Long Island' and Schilling's personal emblem on the engine cowling, Hairless Joe, remained. Note that the radio-equipment was changed: whip antenna was replaced by standard, sword-type, and D/F loop was added. Also note, that the star under starboard wing star is in old style, without bars, and right side's serial in form WW-7938 (without '2'). It is highly probable that sometime later this Thunderbolt was stripped of paint and had a Triangle/H on the yellow horizontal line situated on the vertical tail.

P-47D-5-RE s/n 42-8522, former 353rd FG SX*U Betsy, used as formation monitor by the 92nd BG, Podington, 1945. The whole plane is natural metal colour. On the vertical tail there is a Triangle/B situated on a red horizon-tal line. The plane has an additional 'star and stripes' on the lower surface of the port wing. Note that the aircraft lacks its machine-guns and gunsight, but was fitted with D/F loop and a modified canopy, a 'Malcolm Hood'.

B-17E s/n 41-9020 Phillis, sometime in August/September 1942, when she was assigned to the 92nd BG and was employed as a long-range courier and made several courier flights to North Africa. Note absence of upper turret. Later 'Phillis' was reassigned to the HQ of 303rd BG and renamed 'Tugboat Annie'.

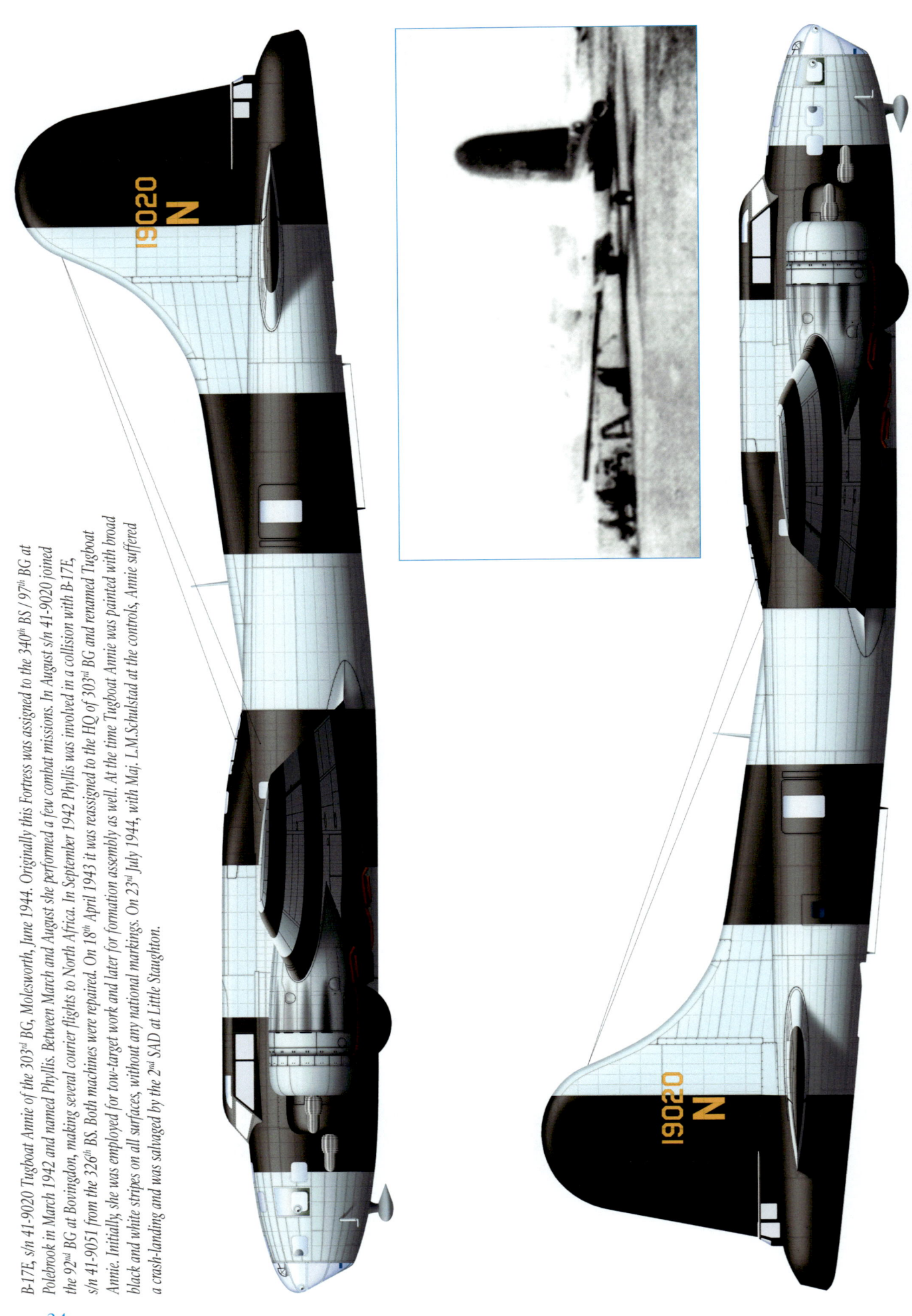

B-17E s/n 41-9020 Tugboat Annie of the 303rd BG, Molesworth, June 1944. Originally this Fortress was assigned to the 340th BS / 97th BG at Polebrook in March 1942 and named Phyllis. Between March and August she performed a few combat missions. In August 41-9020 joined the 92nd BG at Bovingdon, making several courier flights to North Africa. In September 1942 Phyllis was involved in a collision with B-17E, s/n 41-9051 from the 326th BS. Both machines were repaired. On 18th April 1943 it was reassigned to the HQ of 303rd BG and renamed Tugboat Annie. Initially, she was employed for tow-target work and later for formation assembly as well. At the time Tugboat Annie was painted with broad black and white stripes on all surfaces, without any national markings. On 23rd July 1944, with Maj. L.M.Schulstad at the controls, Annie suffered a crash-landing and was salvaged by the 2nd SAD at Little Staughton.

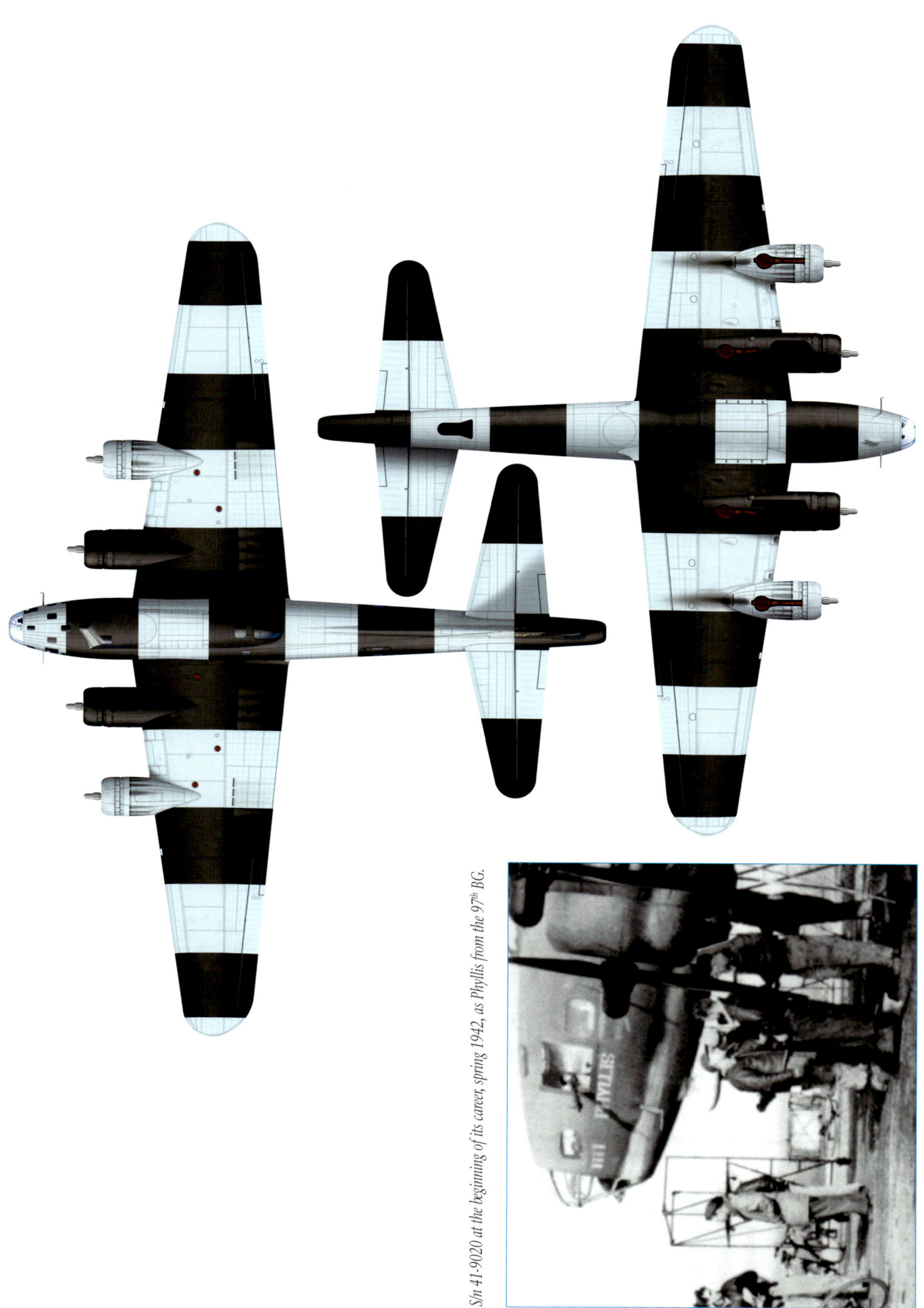

S/n 41-9020 at the beginning of its career, spring 1942, as Phyllis from the 97th BG.

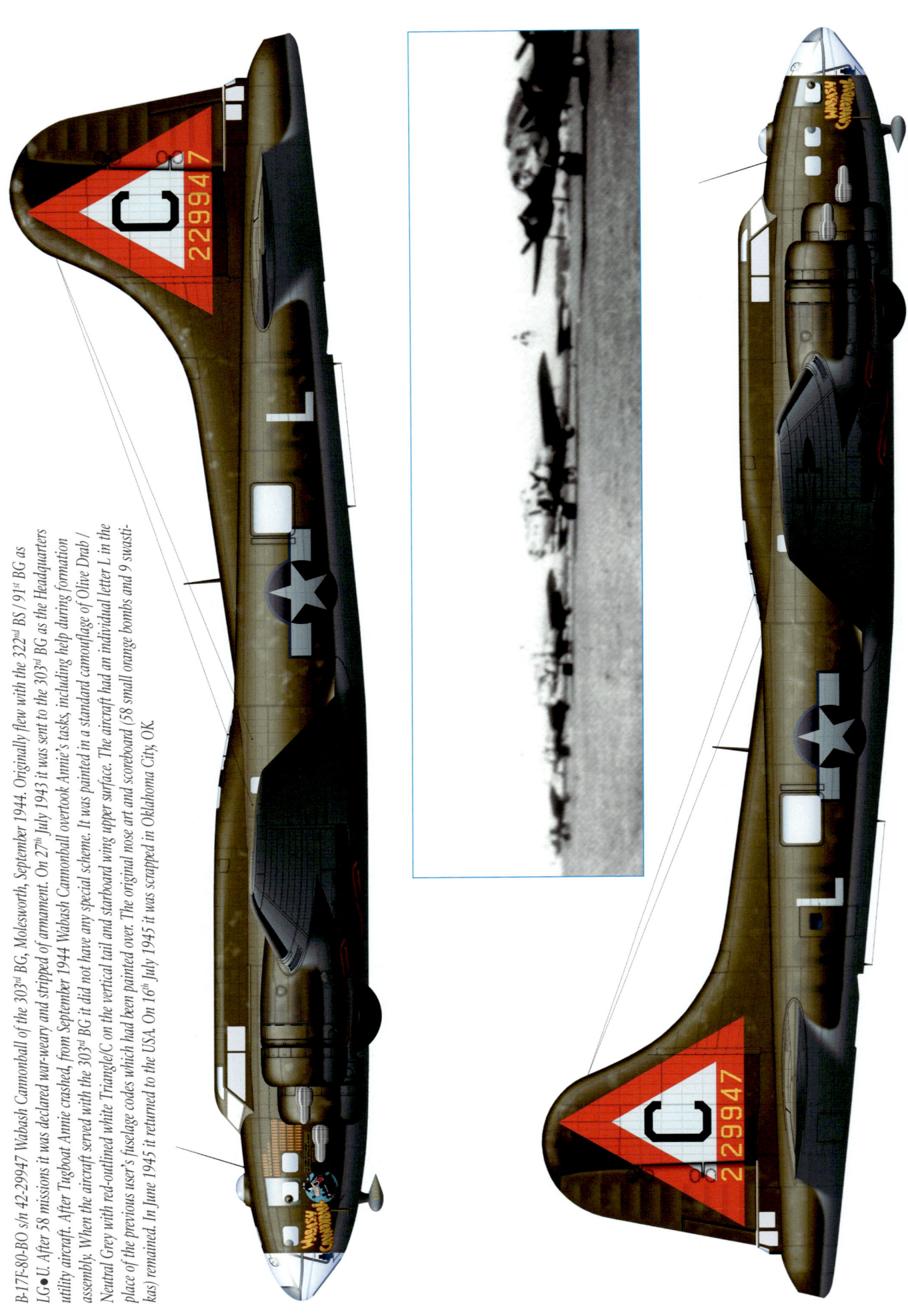

B-17F-80-BO s/n 42-29947 Wabash Cannonball of the 303rd BG, Molesworth, September 1944. Originally flew with the 322nd BS / 91st BG as LG•U. After 58 missions it was declared war-weary and stripped of armament. On 27th July 1943 it was sent to the 303rd BG as the Headquarters utility aircraft. After Tugboat Annie crashed, from September 1944 Wabash Cannonball overtook Annie's tasks, including help during formation assembly. When the aircraft served with the 303rd BG it did not have any special scheme. It was painted in a standard camouflage of Olive Drab / Neutral Grey with red-outlined white Triangle/C on the vertical tail and starboard wing upper surface. The aircraft had an individual letter L in the place of the previous user's fuselage codes which had been painted over. The original nose art and scoreboard (58 small orange bombs and 9 swastikas) remained. In June 1945 it returned to the USA. On 16th July 1945 it was scrapped in Oklahoma City, OK

Colour picture of Wabash Cannonball's nose-art.

Thunderbolt assigned as formation monitor to the 41st CBW, P-47D-5-RE s/n 42-8567, later named as 'The Snoop'

P-47D-5-RE s/n 42-8567 The Snoop, assigned to the 41st CBW at Molesworth. The machine was used by the 303rd BG Headquarters as a formation monitor from July 1944 to May 1945. Initially, in Olive Drab / Neutral Grey camouflage, in which it was delivered to the unit, it was stripped of paint with paint (except the anti-glare panel) during the autumn of 1944. At the same time the aircraft was given a D/F loop, and on the vertical tail a red-black-yellow concentric triangles representing the 41st CBW were painted. There was also an individual letter Q applied on both sides of a fuselage. Note the white stars on the main wheel hub discs on the early variant.

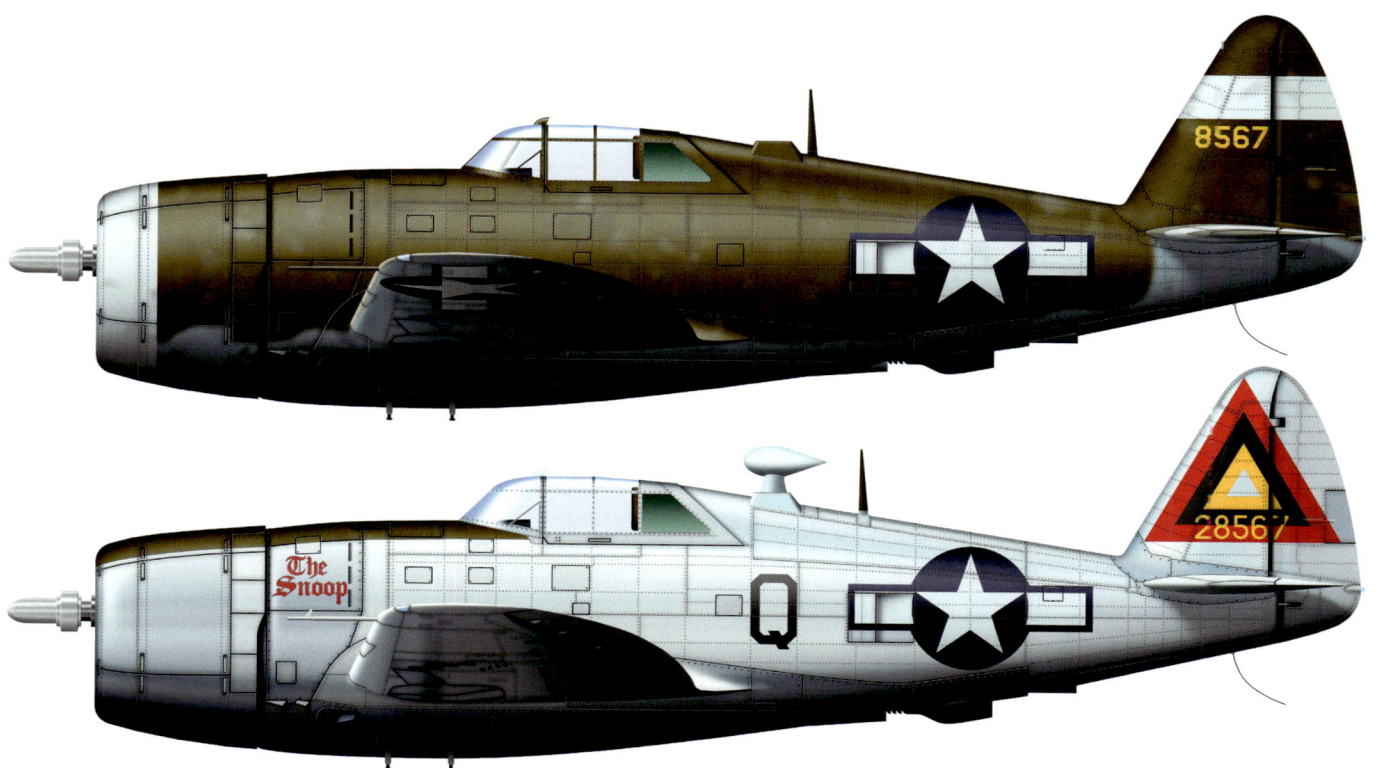

P-47D-11-RE s/n 42-75614 Little Angel, another Thunderbolt which was stationed at Molesworth, but unlike s/n 42-8567 it was assigned directly to the 303rd BG Headquarters from June 1944. Like s/n 42-8526 the aircraft flew as a formation monitor. Initially, in original camouflage in which it was sent to the 303rd BG (including its predecessor's markings, the 486th FS / 352nd FG – PZ●Z), and from the autumn of 1944 had a bare metal with an individual letter R and full set of 303rd BG markings: white triangle outlined in red and a 'C' inside painted on the vertical tail and the upper surface of the starboard wing. It's worth noticing that during removal of the paint the anti-glare panel was left (including the upper part of the engine cowling and windscreen frames), and all the insignia was refreshed. The picture bottom and artwork on the opposite side (upper) show that moment, when there were neither white stars nor white stripes painted on the fuselage. It was temporary only before white paint was added. Note also absence of serial and name, painted just some hours(?) later.

Sgt William R. Weaver (Ground Crew), T/Sgt James R. Welch (Flight Engineer) and T/Sgt James E. Wylde (Squadron Operations) from 303rd BG in front of P-47D-11-RE s/n 42-75614 (later known as) Little Angel.

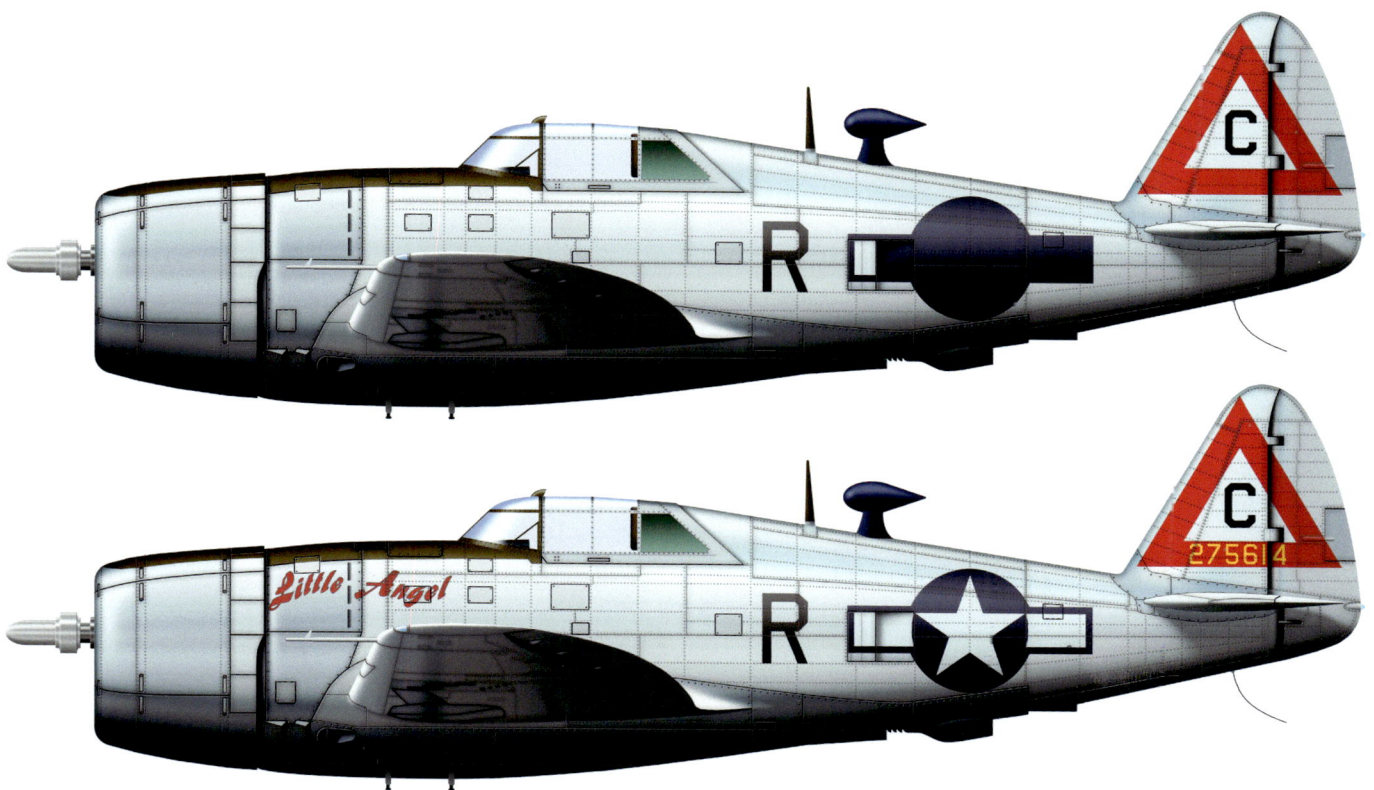

41

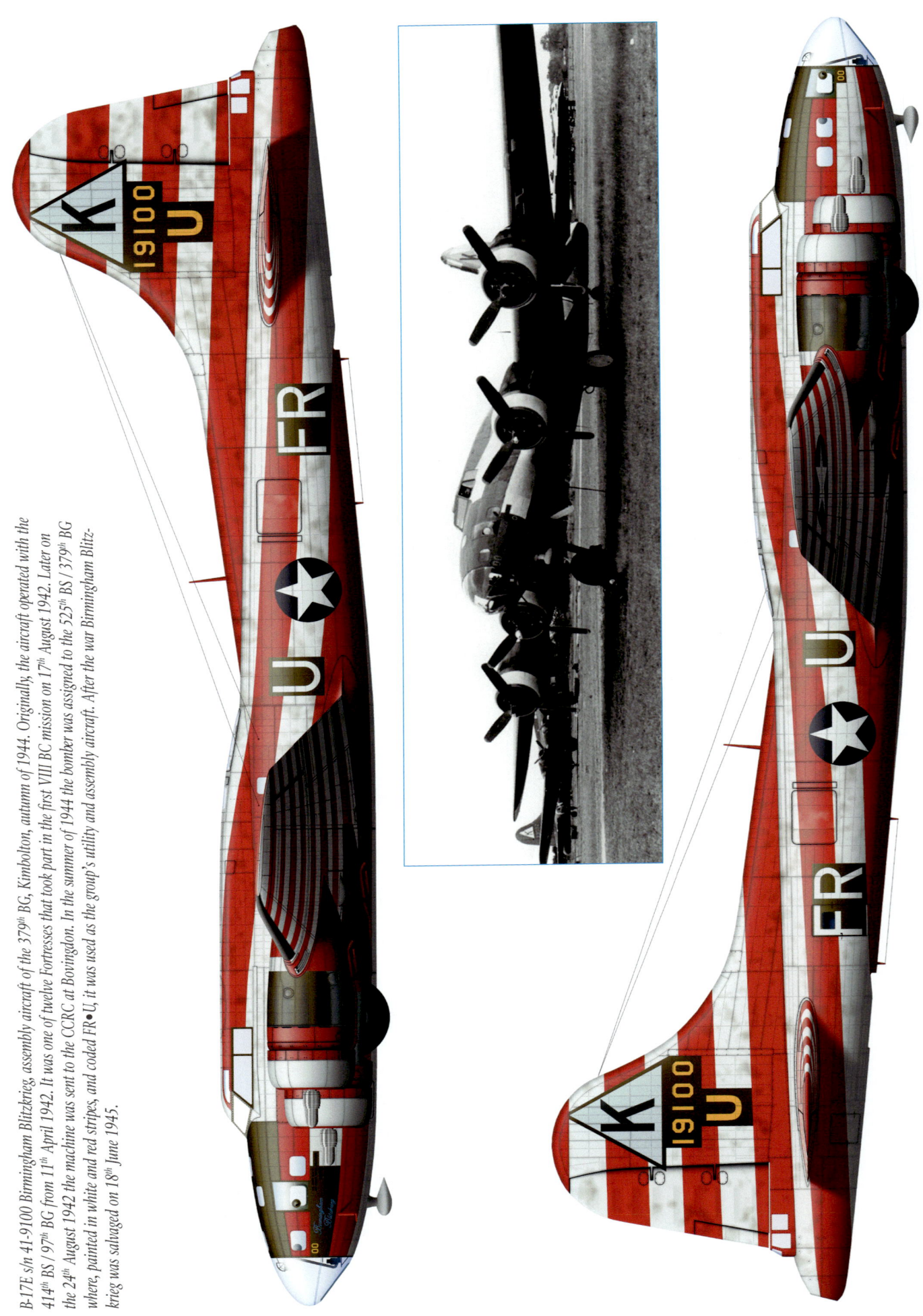

B-17E s/n 41-9100 Birmingham Blitzkrieg assembly aircraft of the 379th BG, Kimbolton, autumn of 1944. Originally, the aircraft operated with the 414th BS / 97th BG from 11th April 1942. It was one of twelve Fortresses that took part in the first VIII BC mission on 17th August 1942. Later on the 24th August 1942 the machine was sent to the CCRC at Bovingdon. In the summer of 1944 the bomber was assigned to the 525th BS / 379th BG where, painted in white and red stripes, and coded FR•U, it was used as the group's utility and assembly aircraft. After the war Birmingham Blitzkrieg was salvaged on 18th June 1945.

B-17E s/n 41-9100 'Birmingham Blitzkrieg' as one of the bombers of the 97th BG, that took part in the very first raid of the Mighty Eighth at Rouen on the 17th August 1942.

Another pictures of Birmingham Blitzkrieg.

P-47D-10-RE s/n 42-75154, formation monitor of the 384th BG, Grafton Underwood, 1945. The whole aircraft is natural metal overall. The vertical tail was given a white triangle with a black outline and the letter 'P' inside. The aircraft lacks machine-guns, gunsight, and armoured glass. However, it is fitted with underwing racks. Note that the serial number was painted incorrectly.

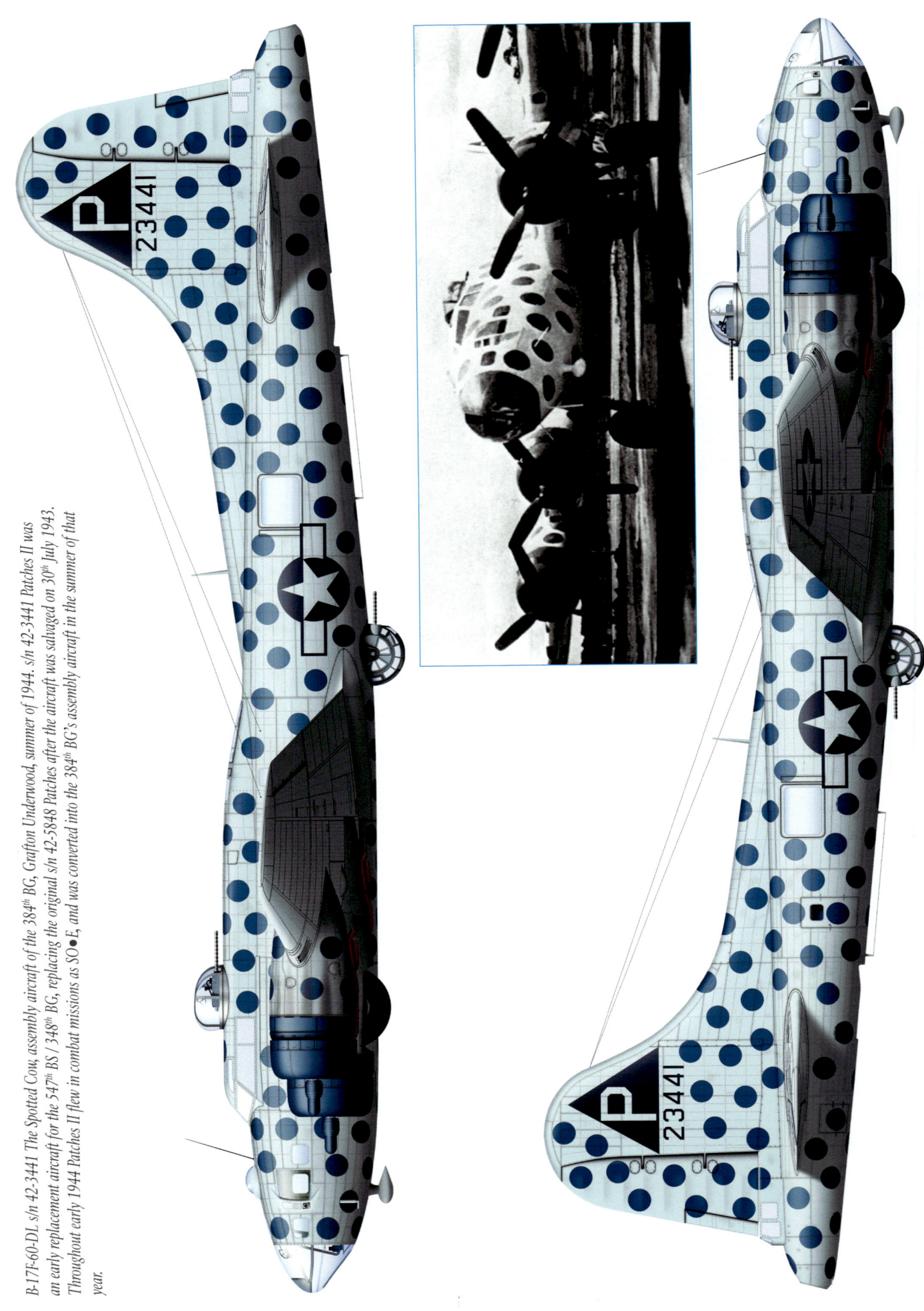

B-17F-60-DL s/n 42-3441 The Spotted Cow, assembly aircraft of the 384th BG, Grafton Underwood, summer of 1944. s/n 42-3441 Patches II was an early replacement aircraft for the 547th BS / 348th BG, replacing the original s/n 42-5848 Patches after the aircraft was salvaged on 30th July 1943. Throughout early 1944 Patches II flew in combat missions as SO●E, and was converted into the 384th BG's assembly aircraft in the summer of that year.

The aircraft was given a high-visibility blue polka dot design on all surfaces (except the under surfaces) painted previously in white and immediately after she was given a new look she was nicknamed Spotted Cow. On the vertical tail and the starboard wing upper surface a dark-blue triangle with a white 'P' within were applied. The engine cowlings and the propeller hubs were painted the same blue as the polka dots. Note that the aircraft was only partially disarmed; the armament in the top and ventral turrets was left and the turrets remained in their original colors, the upper being natural metal and the ventral Neutral Grey.

351st BG Lucky Strike with Lt. J. Wroblewski and crew.
One mare shot taken at Kingman, shown a fragment of The Black Bitch on right background.

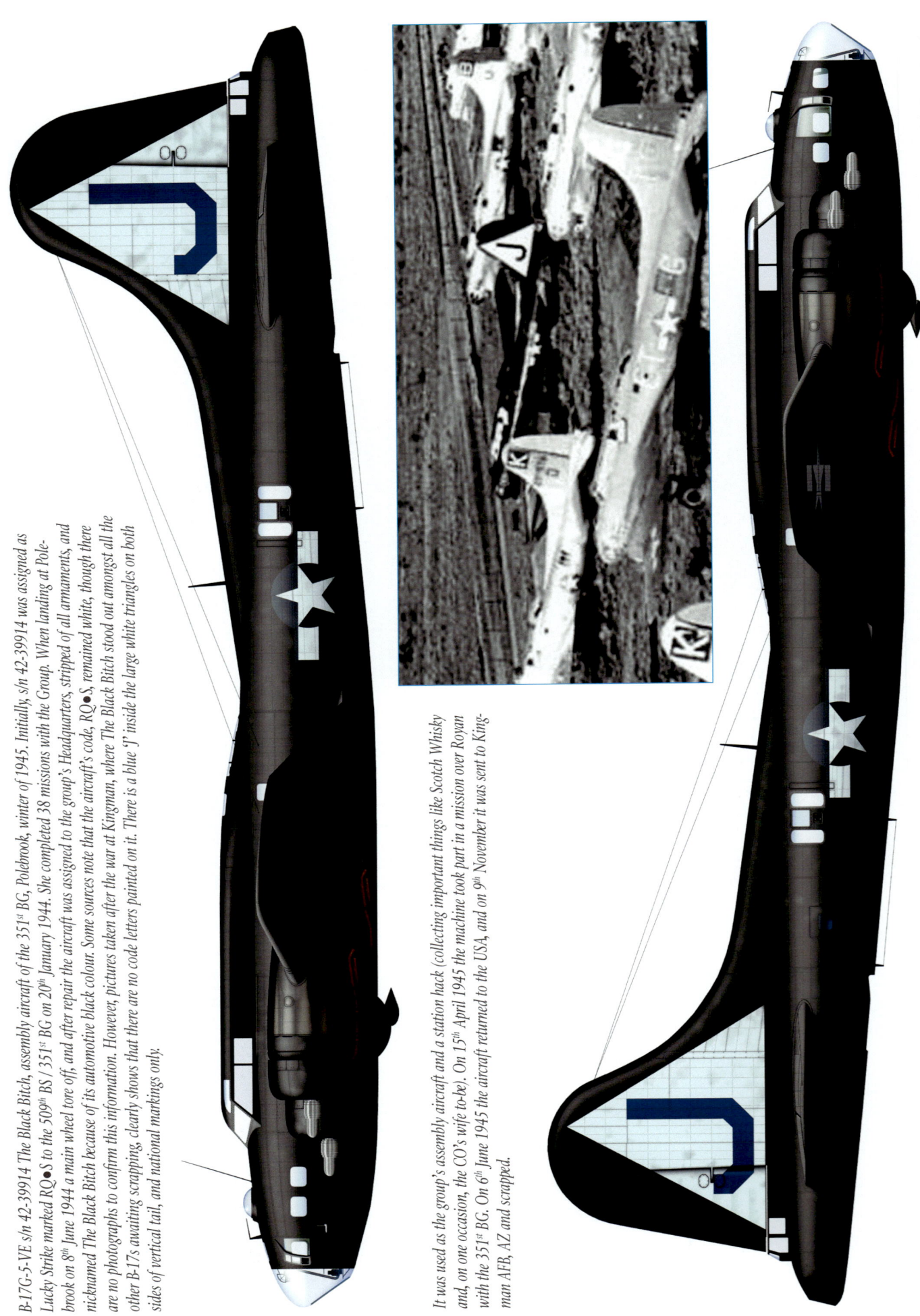

B-17G-5-VE s/n 42-39914 The Black Bitch, assembly aircraft of the 351st BG, Polebrook, winter of 1945. Initially, s/n 42-39914 was assigned as Lucky Strike marked RQ●S to the 509th BS / 351st BG on 20th January 1944. She completed 38 missions with the Group. When landing at Polebrook on 8th June 1944 a main wheel tore off, and after repair the aircraft was assigned to the group's Headquarters, stripped of all armaments, and nicknamed The Black Bitch because of its automotive black colour. Some sources note that the aircraft's code, RQ●S, remained white, though there are no photographs to confirm this information. However, pictures taken after the war at Kingman, where The Black Bitch stood out amongst all the other B-17s awaiting scrapping, clearly shows that there are no code letters painted on it. There is a blue 'J' inside the large white triangles on both sides of vertical tail, and national markings only.

It was used as the group's assembly aircraft and a station hack (collecting important things like Scotch Whisky and, on one occasion, the CO's wife to-be). On 15th April 1945 the machine took part in a mission over Royan with the 351st BG. On 6th June 1945 the aircraft returned to the USA, and on 9th November it was sent to Kingman AFB, AZ and scrapped.

Nose section and the crew of Lucky Strike. Polebrook, spring of 1944.

Another shot of The Black Bitch at Kingman. In the foreground s/n 42-97976 A Bit O' Lace of the 709th BS/447th BG.

P-47D-2-RE s/n 42-8226, formation monitor of the 401st BG, Deenethorpe, 1945. Originally assigned to the 335th FS / 4th FG as WD●I, where it was flown mainly by Maj. Carpenter. After service in the 4th FG, the machine was reassigned to the 401st BG, where it was used as a formation monitor until the end of the war. Throughout its whole career with the 401st BG, the aircraft had its previous user's markings, but unlike the previous user the aircraft was disarmed.

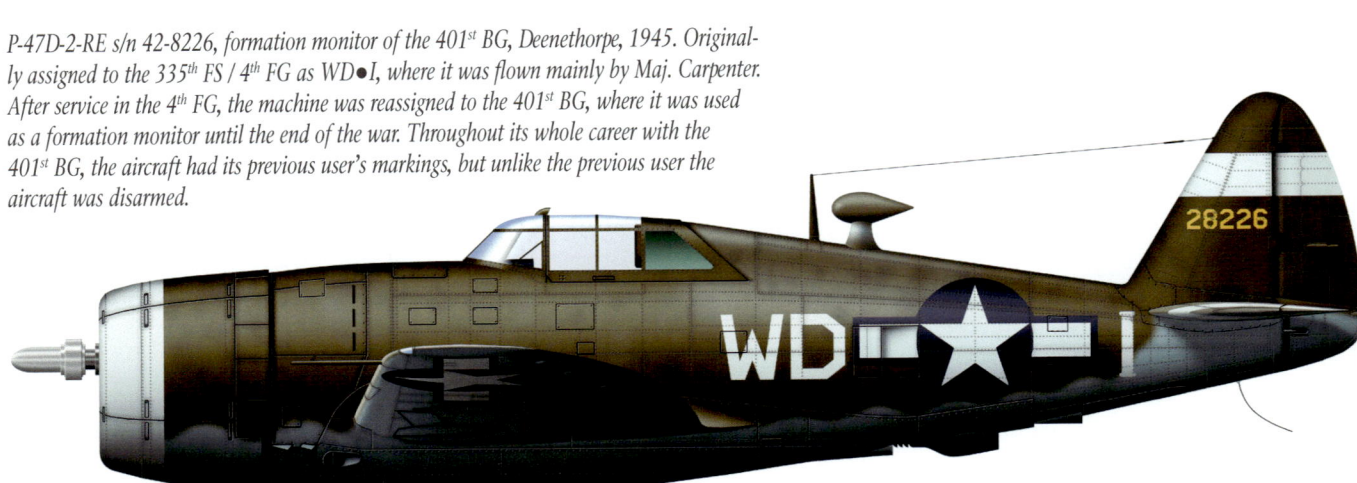

P-47D-11-RE s/n 42-75218. After service with the 61st FS/56th FG as HV●K it was declared War-Weary and used by the 457th BG as the formation monitor. When it was with the 457th BG it still retained armament and the markings of the previous user.

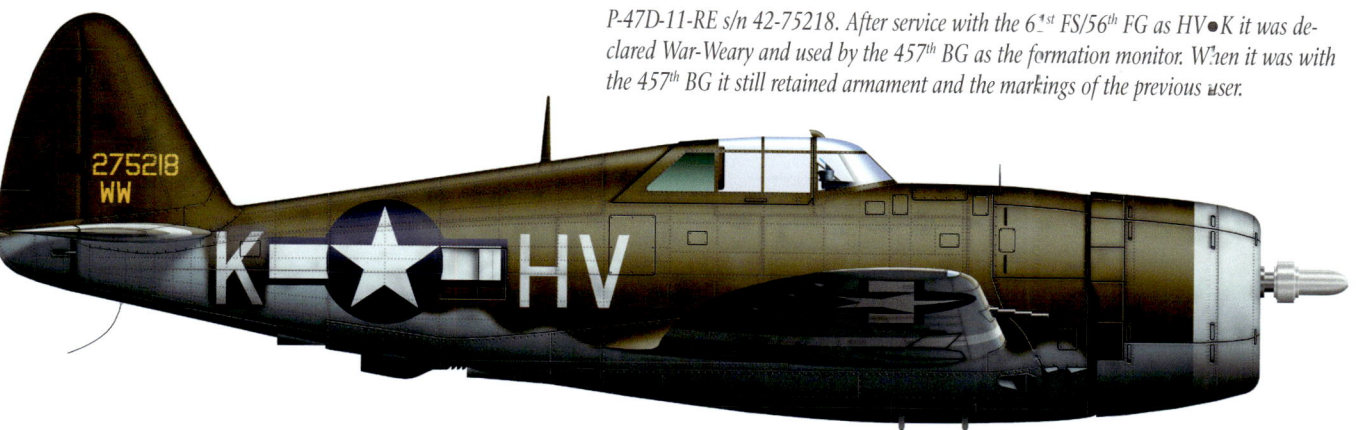

P-47D-22-RE s/n 42-25959. Ex – 56th FG plane, declared War-Weary and assigned for non-combat duties with 2nd Combat Bombardment Wing's Headquarter Flight at Sta.114 / Hethel. Sometimes used as formation monitor for 389th BG. Damaged during landing accident on 14th May 1945 (with S M Meintsma at controls) due to bad weather at Attlebridge, not repaired.

P-47D-5-RE s/n 42-8532, employed as the formation monitor of the 389th BG, Hethel 1944. Note that the serial number was painted on by hand, without a stencil. The aircraft had its armament, gunsight, and armoured glass removed.

P-47D-5-RE s/n 42-8532 in later form after April 1944, when the tail markings was changed for Group's colours.

55

Thunderbolts (s/n 42-8532 & s/n 42-28659), both of 389 BG's formation monitors, together with UC-45 in front of a T-2 Hangar at Hethel, fall 1944.

P-47D-28-RA s/n 42-28659 FAG, the second formation monitor of the 389th BG, Hethel, late 1944. During initial job as monitor, the aircraft keep its armament and gunsight, later removed. The plane was moved for second-line duties from 495th FTG.

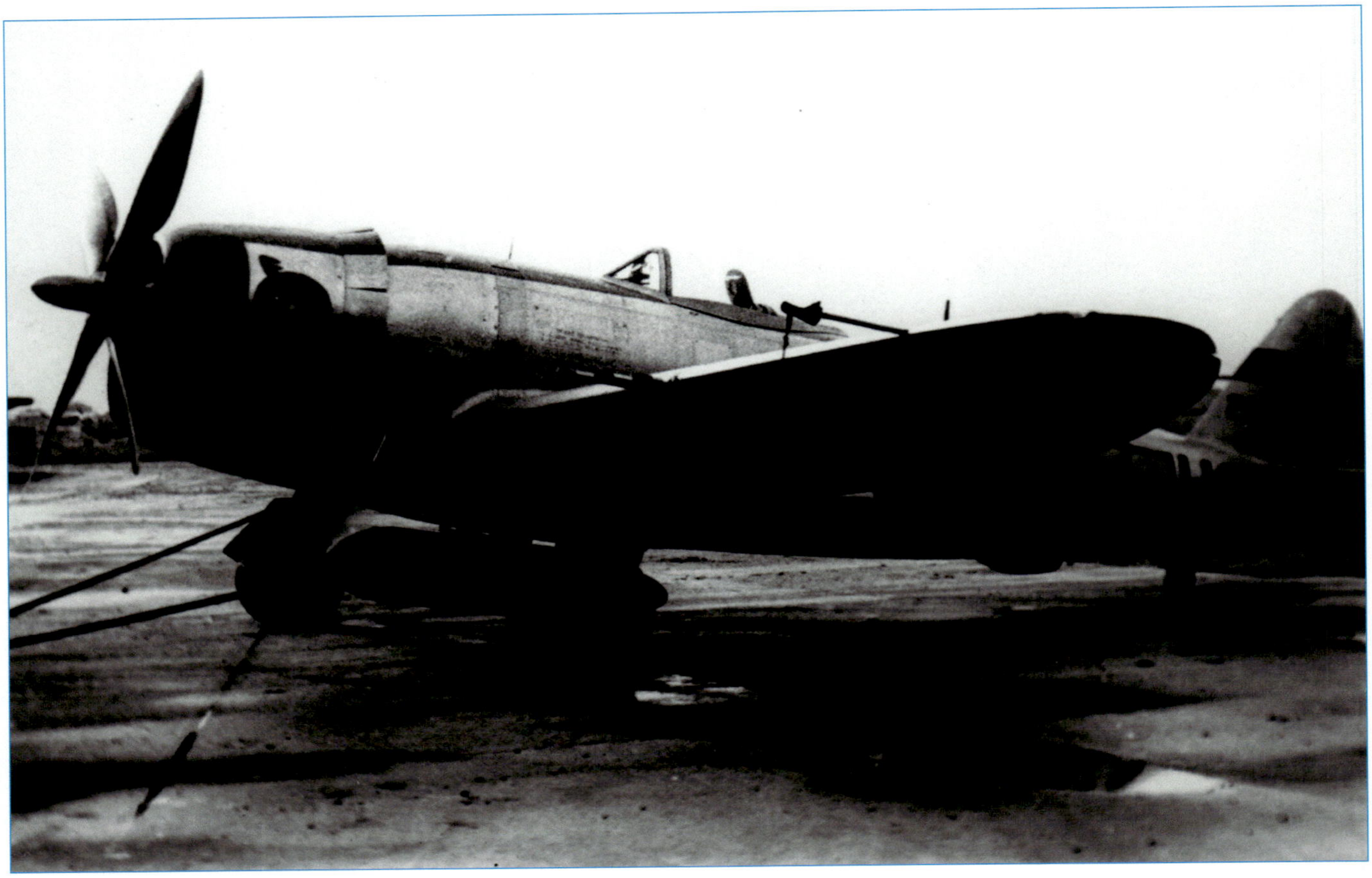

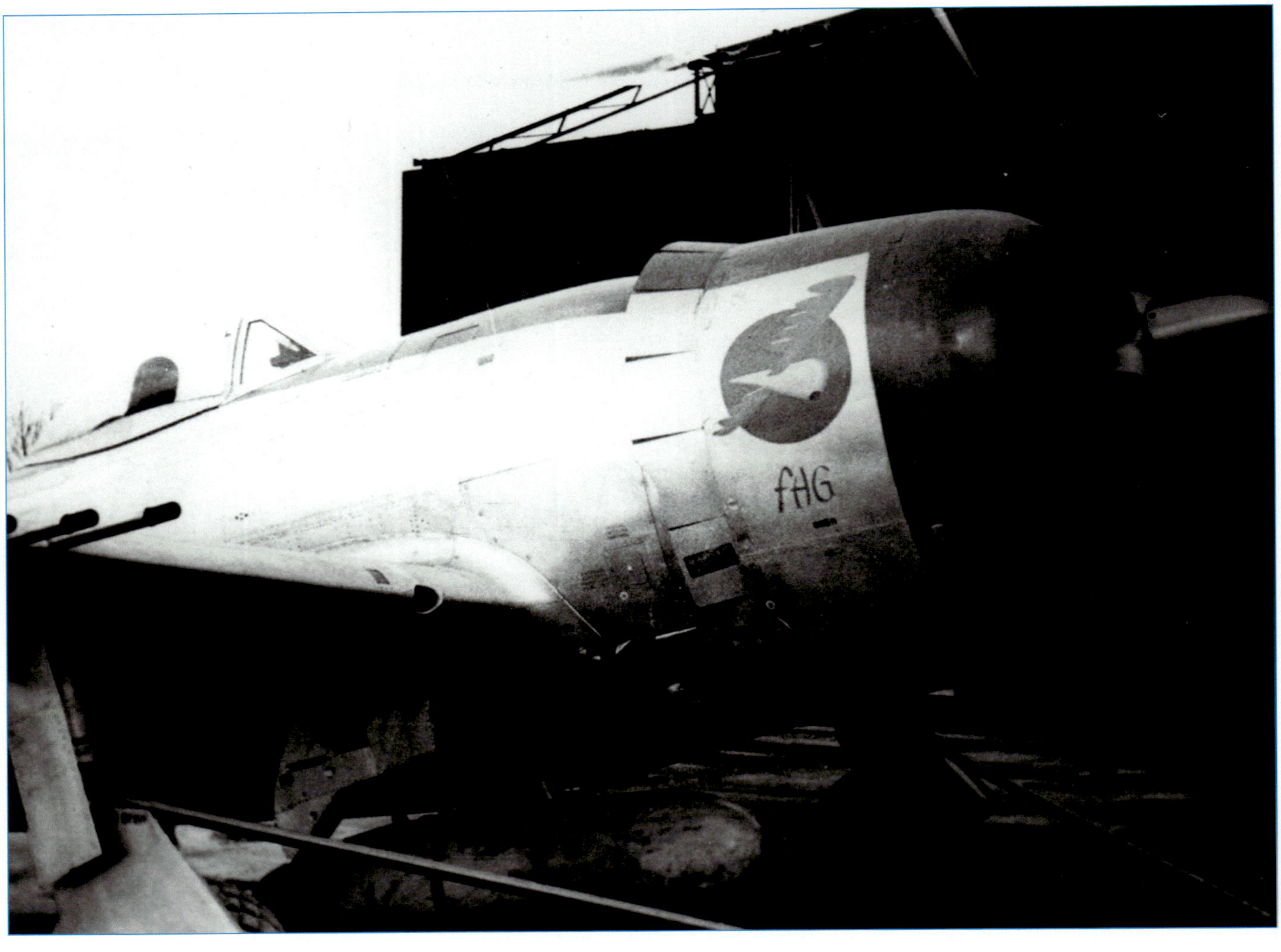
fAG

B-24D-1-CO s/n 41-23683 The Green Dragon, assembly ship of the 389th BG, Hethel, January 1944. The Green Dragon was one of the first aircraft used to help in formation assembly. In December 1943 Jo Jo's Special Delivery was inherited after the 93rd BG relocated from North Africa. The aircraft was stripped of paint and decorated with yellow and green diagonal stripes painted on the fuselage and wings. The inner engine cowlings were green, while the outers were yellow. Initially, when it was known as the "Zebra Forming Aircraft", the aircraft retained its top and rear turret armament. Note the helpful navigation lights mounted in the rear fuselage.

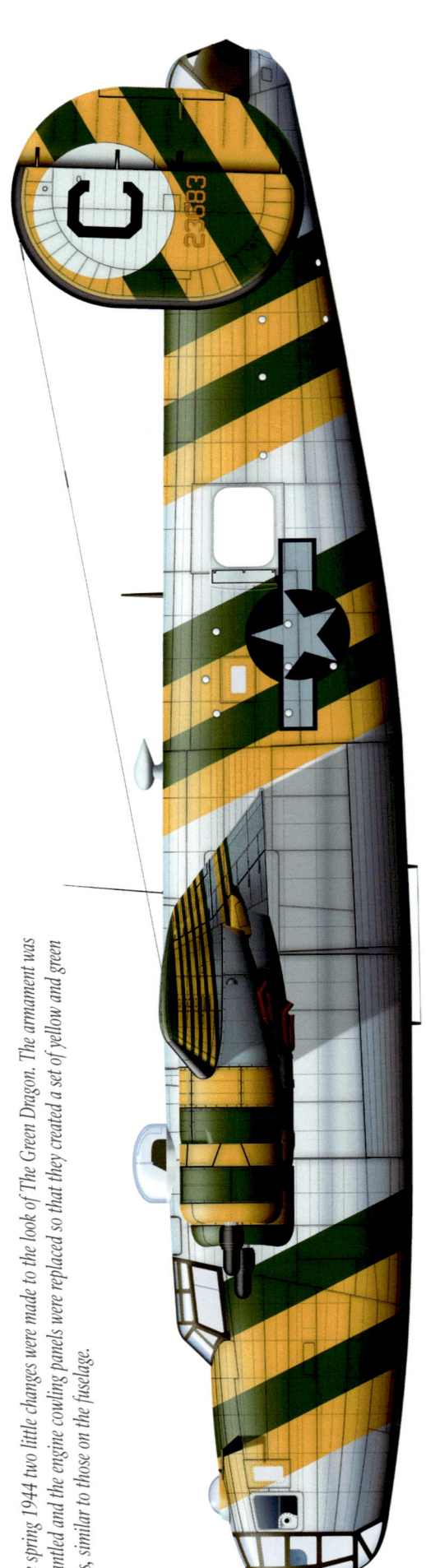

In the spring 1944 two little changes were made to the look of The Green Dragon. The armament was dismantled and the engine cowling panels were replaced so that they created a set of yellow and green stripes, similar to those on the fuselage.

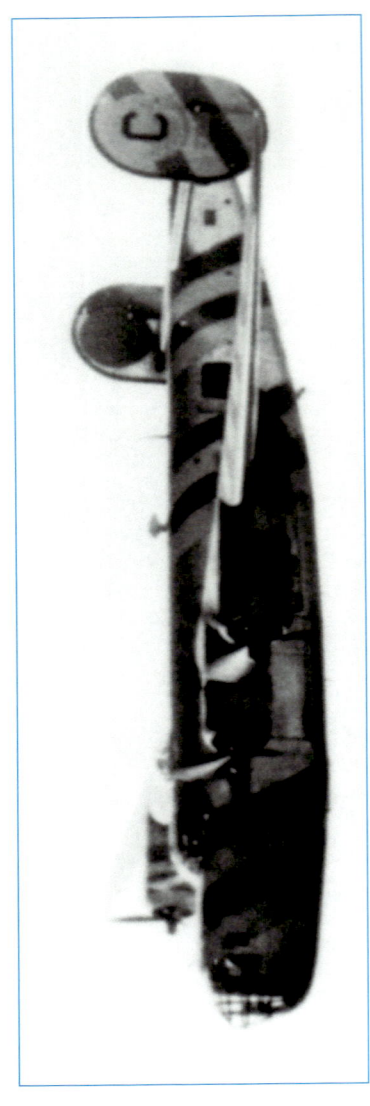

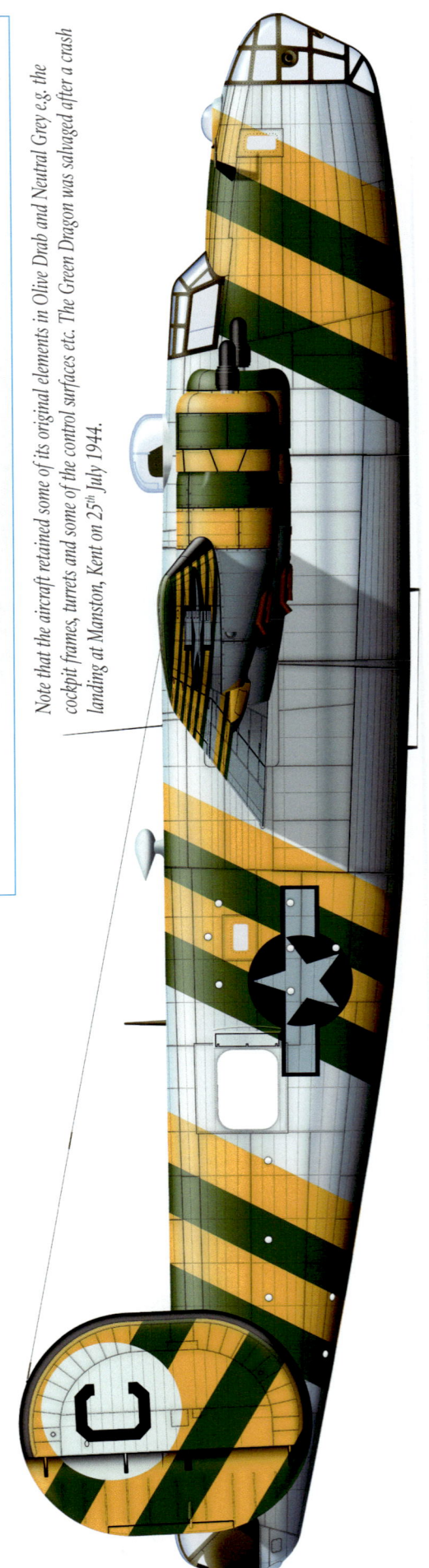

Note that the aircraft retained some of its original elements in Olive Drab and Neutral Grey e.g. the cockpit frames, turrets and some of the control surfaces etc. The Green Dragon was salvaged after a crash landing at Manston, Kent on 25th July 1944.

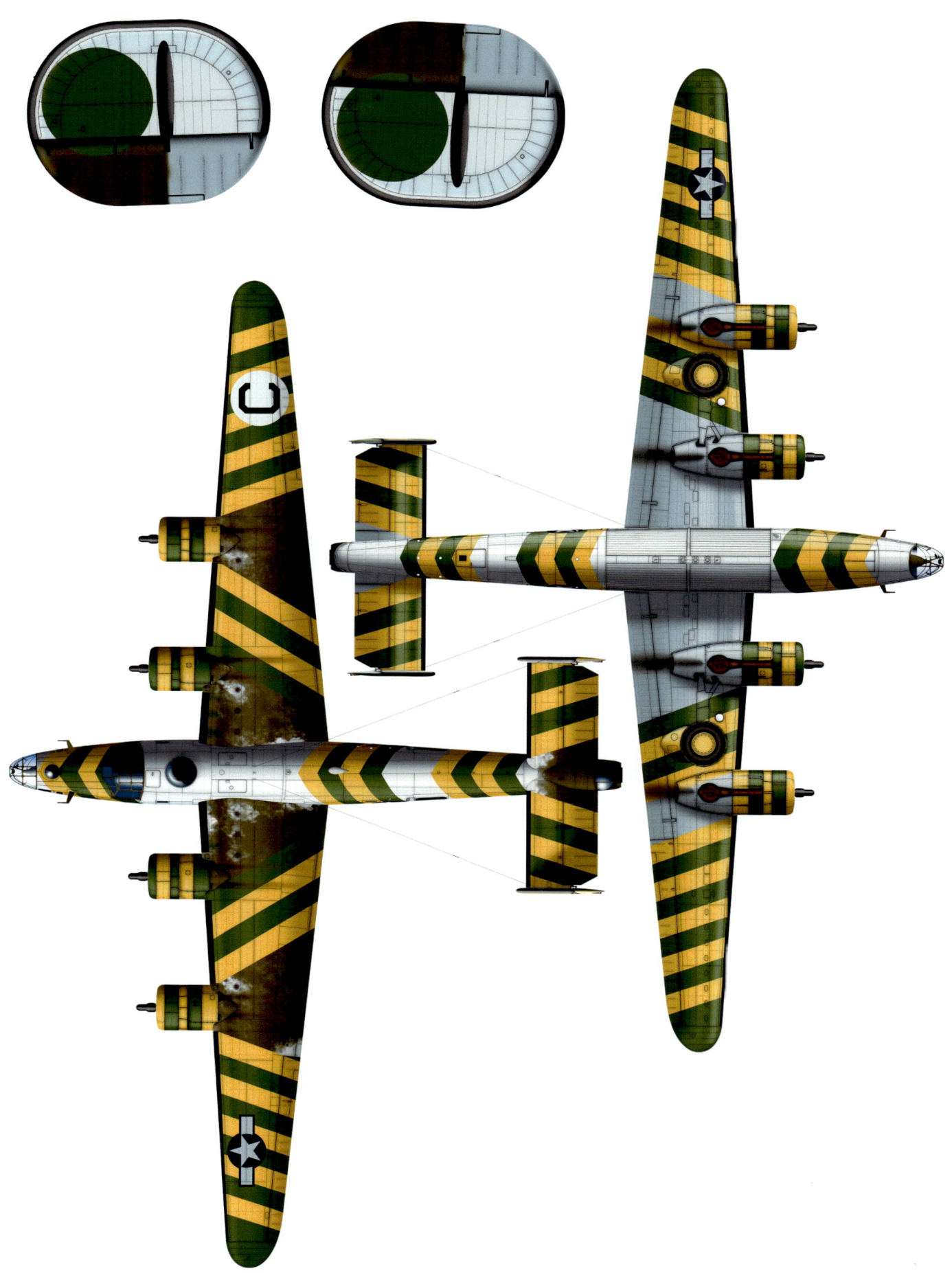

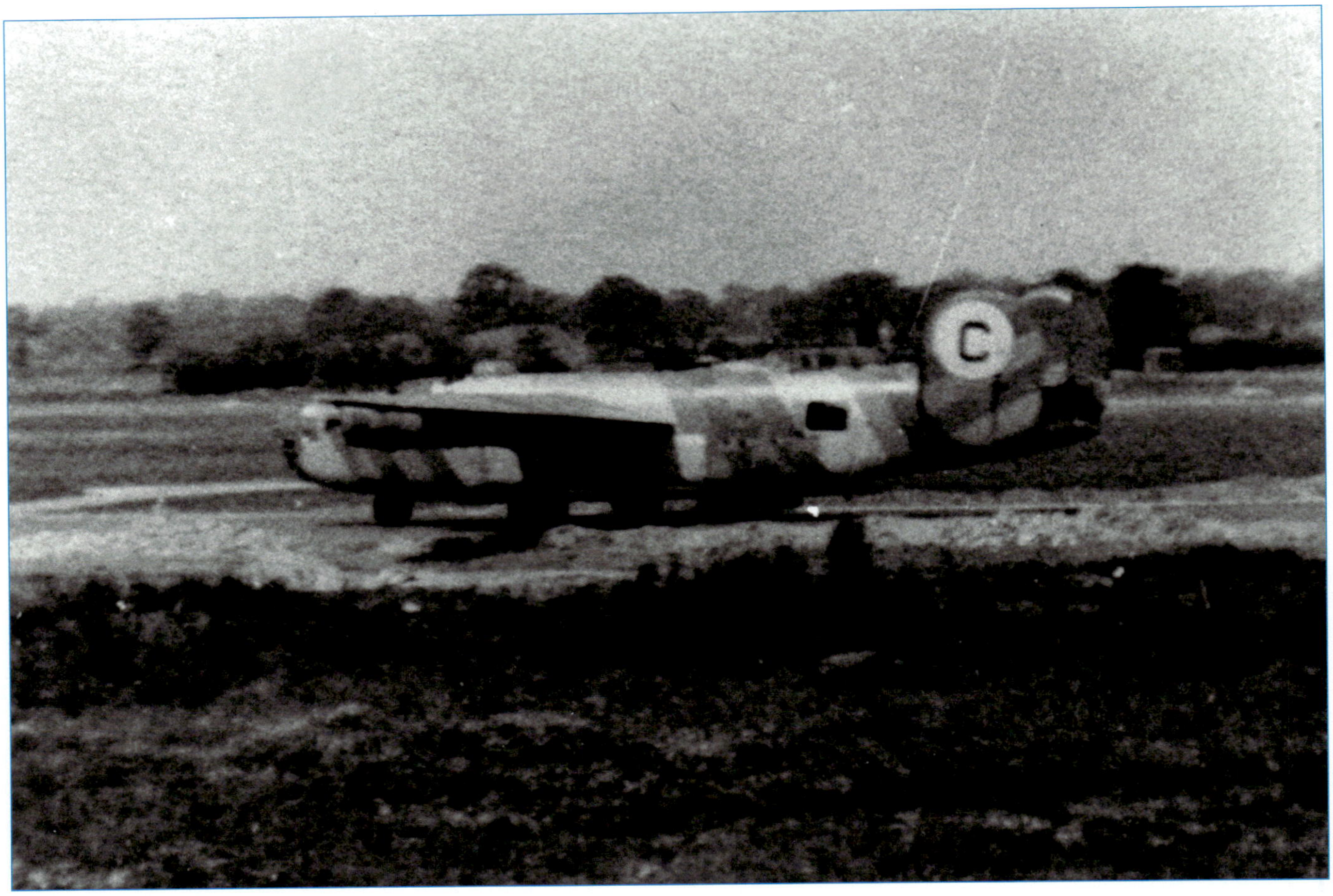
C

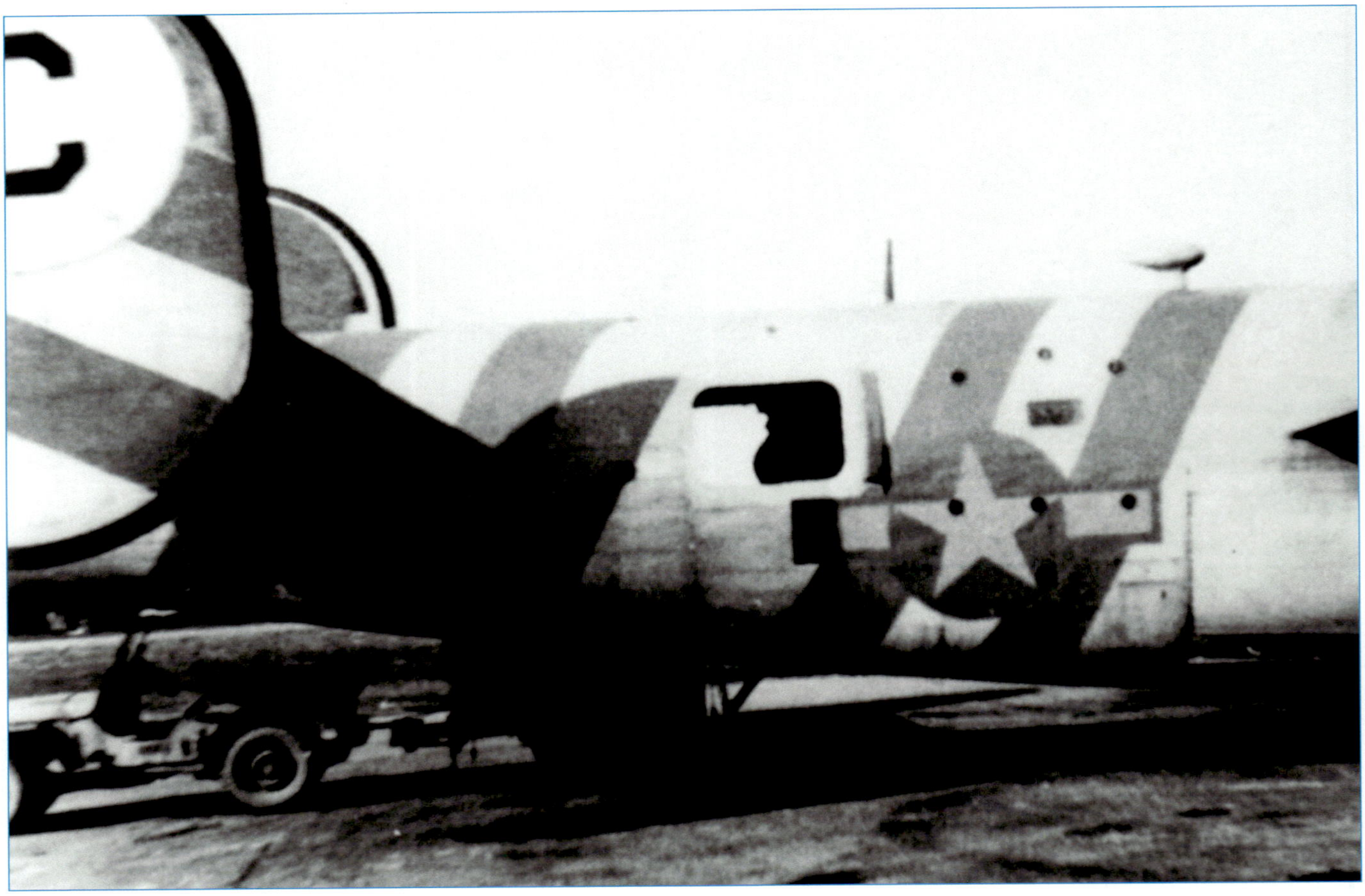
C

*B-24J-55-CO s/n 42-99972 RR*I+ The Sad Sack of 566 BS with modified nose section.*

The same aircraft s/n 42-99972 as The Green Dragon II, a second assembly ship of the 389th BG at Great Ashfield, Summer 1944. Poor in quality, but an important photo on the right shows, that the tail of this Liberator was also painted with pattern of linked squares and individual letter 'C'. Now we can be sure that it was certainty not 'I+' (as it was show in 'A.S.' 1st Ed.).

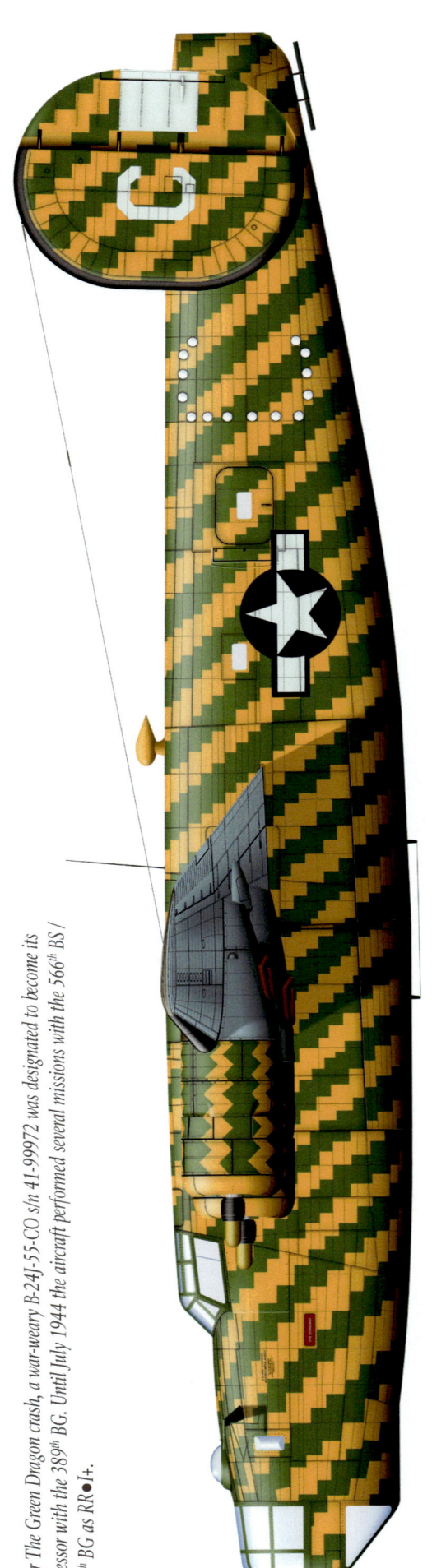

After The Green Dragon crash, a war-weary B-24J-55-CO s/n 41-99972 was designated to become its successor with the 389th BG. Until July 1944 the aircraft performed several missions with the 566th BS / 389th BG as RR•I+.

After the machine was lightened by replacing the turrets with 'glasshouses', the fuselage and the engines were painted in a yellow and green pattern of linked squares. The wings and horizontal tail were left in their original form. It's interesting that the navigator's window on the starboard side of the nose was taken from a B-24M.

B-24J-55-CO s/n 41-99972, assembly ship of the 389th BG in its final form, Hethel, spring of 1945. In early 1945 a decorative motif, eyes and a shark's mouth appeared on the nose of s/n 41-99972, just as on many other Liberators of the 389th BG. The eye painted on the starboard side is painted differently from that on the port side because of the panel of the navigator's window taken from a B-24M. Also the individual letter I+ on the outer surfaces of the vertical fin was painted over.

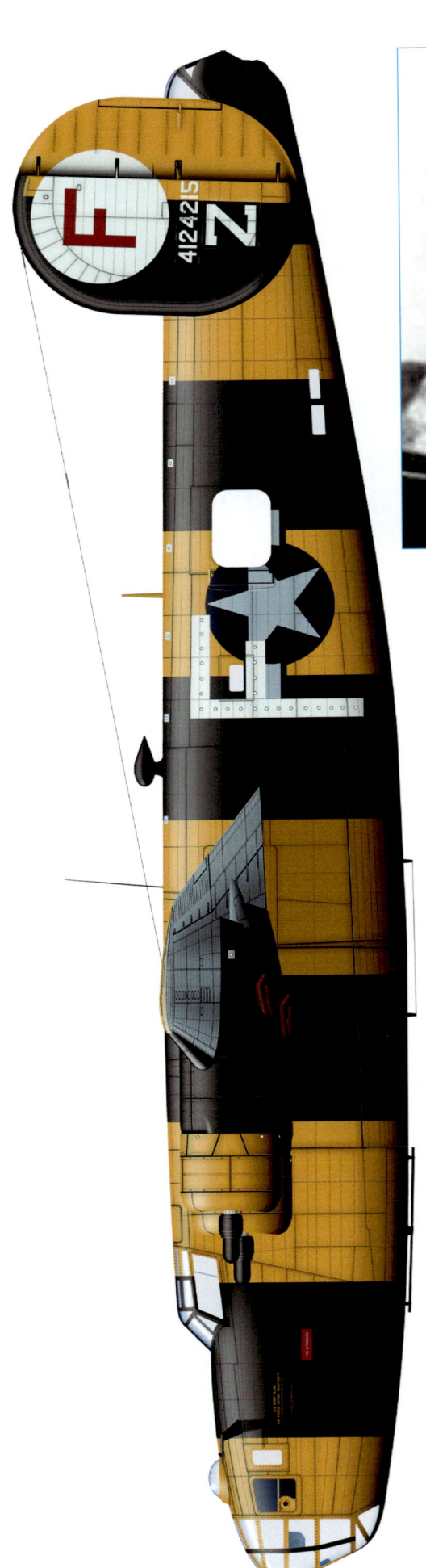
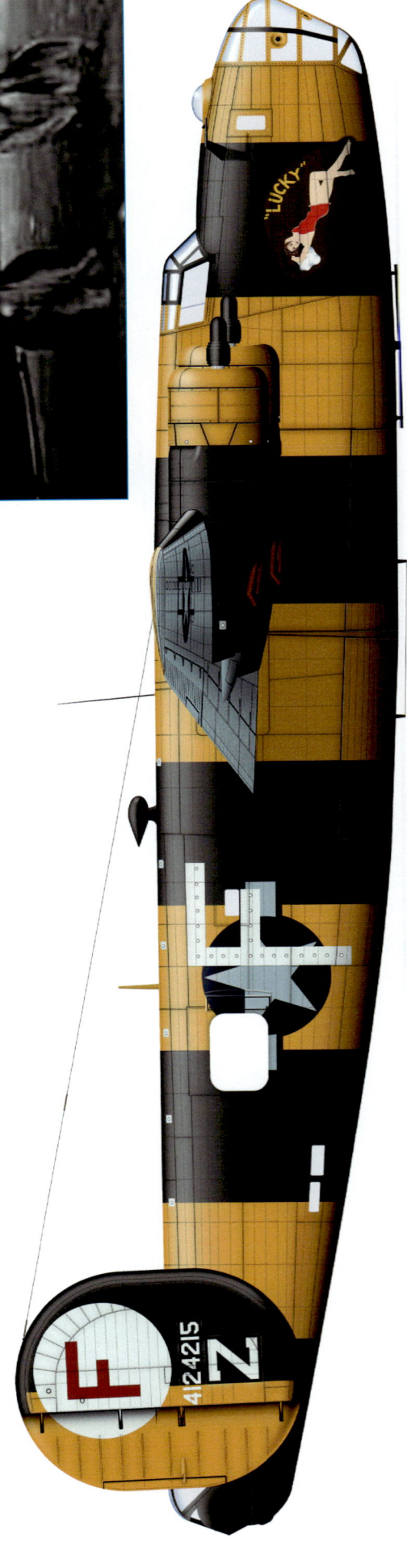

B-24D-20-CO s/n 41-24215 Lucky Gordon, assembly ship of the 445th BG, Tibenham, January 1944. Following its retirement in the 93rd BG, Lucky Gordon was transferred to the 445th BG where it became that group's first assembly ship. The machine, in its new role, was stripped of armament and painted in contrasting orange and black colours with the exception of the wing and horizontal tail undersurfaces. A large white letter 'F', with small navigational lights inside, was applied on both sides of the fuselage. Additional lines of lights were added on the top of the fuselage. The aircraft retained its original nose art on the starboard side of the nose. Note that the serial number was painted in an incorrect style. On several occasions Lucky Gordon led the group beyond the English Channel. In 1944 Lucky Gordon was replaced by an unknown natural metal-finished B-24H, the serial number of which the author has been unable to confirm.

Hap Kendal (right) and C.S. Young before Ploesti mission. Note "Lucky's" pin-up girl nose-art as a background.

B-24D-20-CO s/n 41-24215 *Lucky* before it became an assembly ship.

P-47D-11-RE s/n 42-2983, employed as the formation monitor of the 445th BG, Tibenham, 1944.

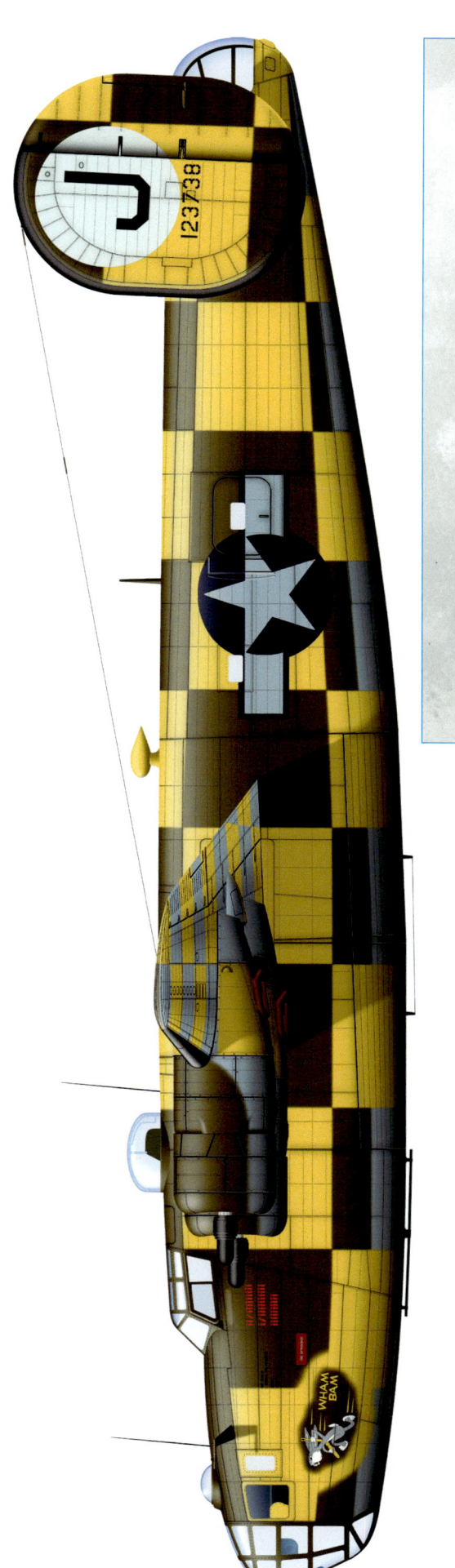
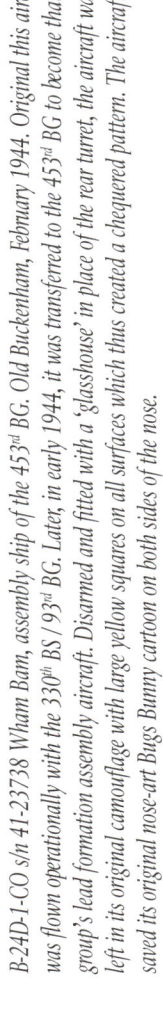
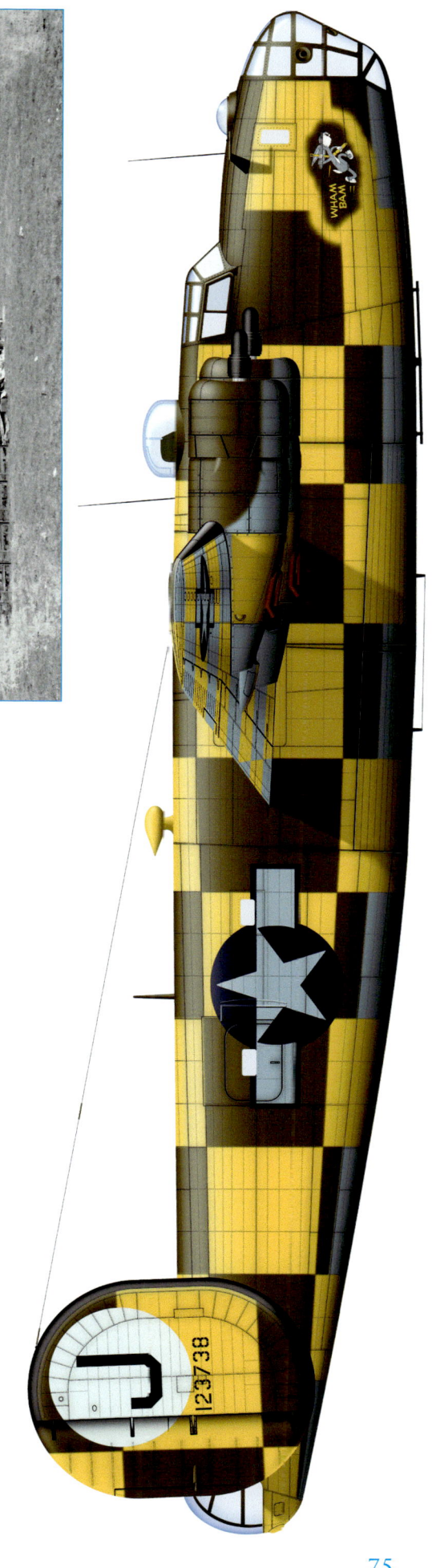

B-24D-1-CO s/n 41-23738 Wham Bam, assembly ship of the 453rd BG, Old Buckenham, February 1944. Original this aircraft was flown operationally with the 330th BS / 93rd BG. Later, in early 1944, it was transferred to the 453rd BG to become that group's lead formation assembly aircraft. Disarmed and fitted with a 'glasshouse' in place of the rear turret, the aircraft was left in its original camouflage with large yellow squares on all surfaces which thus created a chequered pattern. The aircraft saved its original nose-art Bugs Bunny cartoon on both sides of the nose.

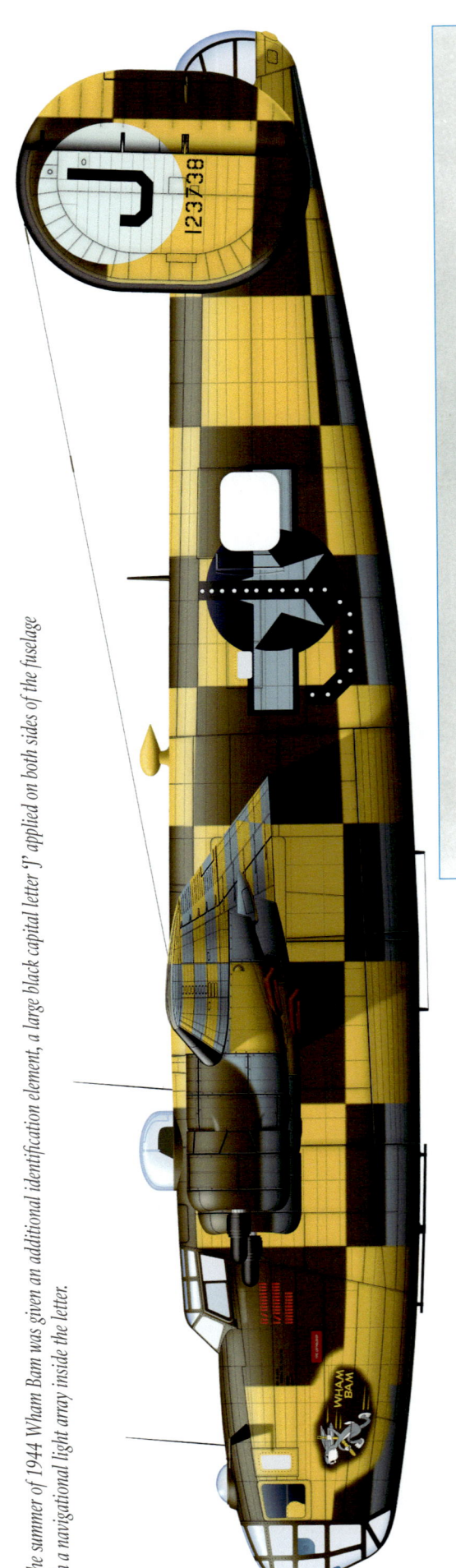

In the summer of 1944 Wham Bam was given an additional identification element, a large black capital letter 'J' applied on both sides of the fuselage with a navigational light array inside the letter.

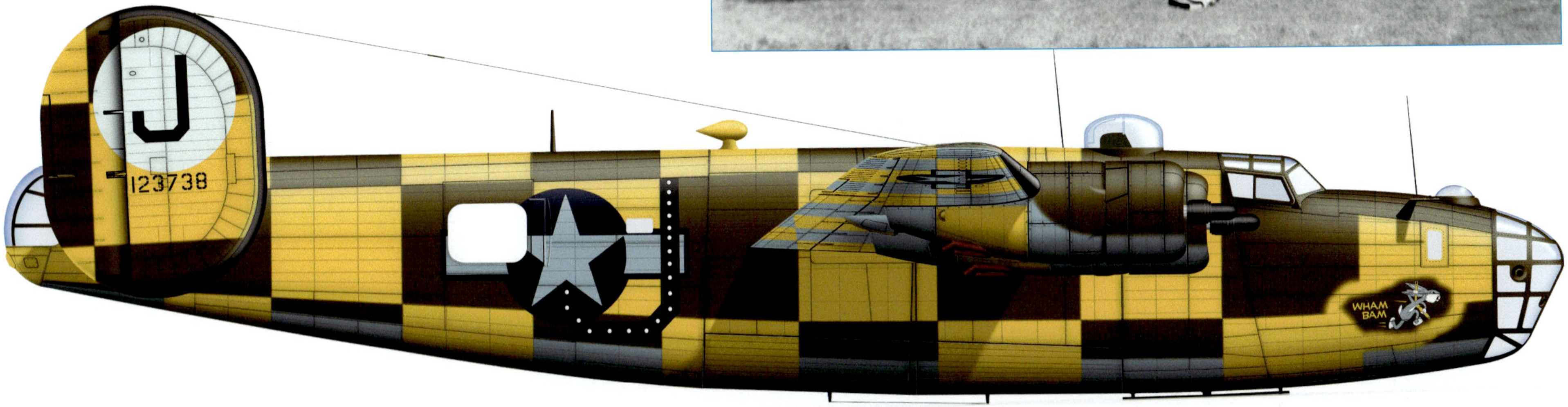

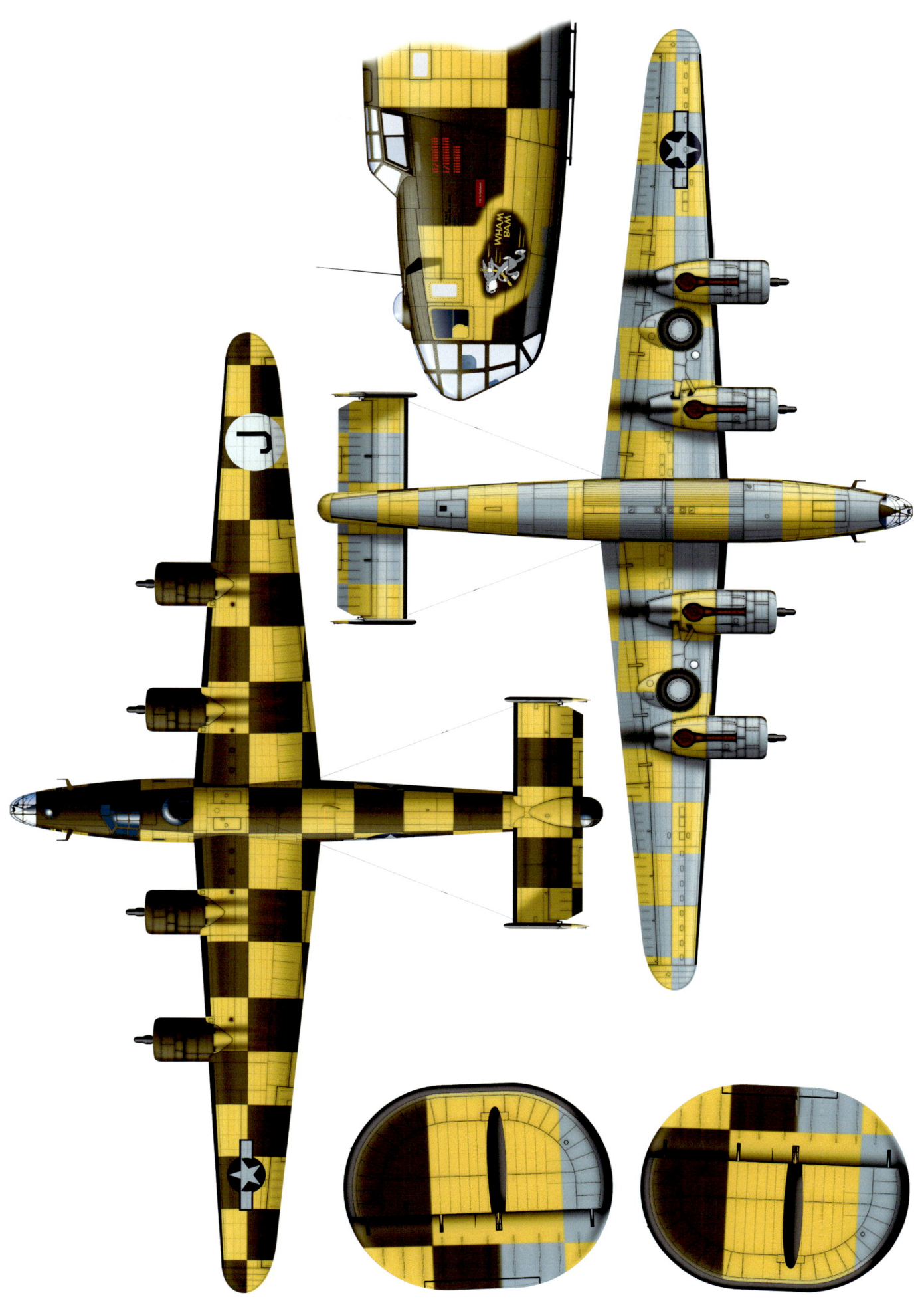

WHAM
BAM

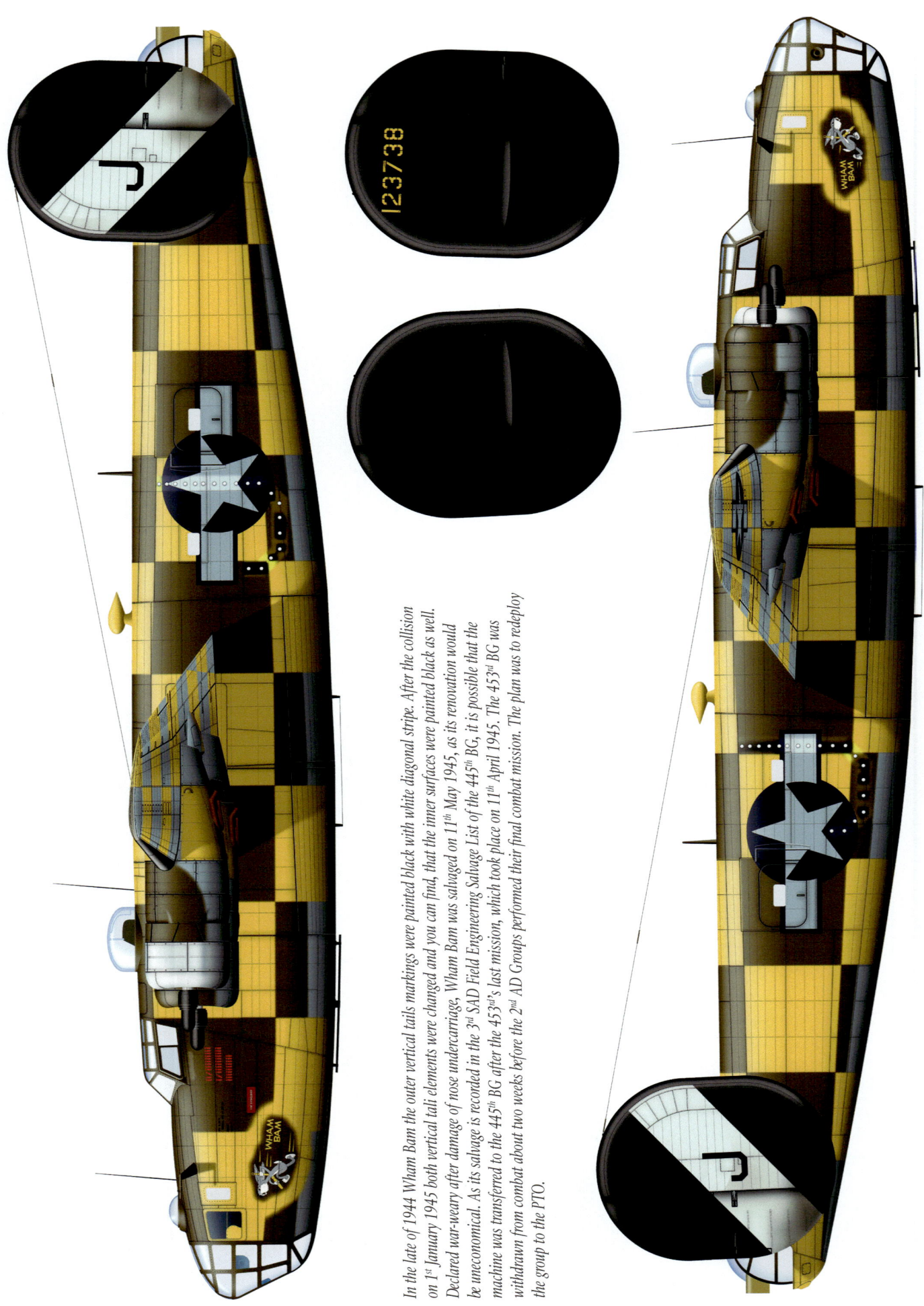

In the late of 1944 Wham Bam the outer vertical tails markings were painted black with white diagonal stripe. After the collision on 1st January 1945 both vertical tail elements were changed and you can find, that the inner surfaces were painted black as well. Declared war-weary after damage of nose undercarriage, Wham Bam was salvaged on 11th May 1945, as its renovation would be uneconomical. As its salvage is recorded in the 3rd SAD Field Engineering Salvage List of the 445th BG, it is possible that the machine was transferred to the 445th BG after the 453rd's last mission, which took place on 11th April 1945. The 453rd BG was withdrawn from combat about two weeks before the 2nd AD Groups performed their final combat mission. The plan was to redeploy the group to the PTO.

P-47C-5-RE s/n 41-6630, formation monitor of the 453rd BG. Old Buckenham, winter of 1945. The whole machine was stripped of paint, except for a short anti-glare panel, wing root panels and the vertical tail which were painted black. Diagonal bands on the vertical tail were left unpainted, but the letter 'J' was applied on white discs.

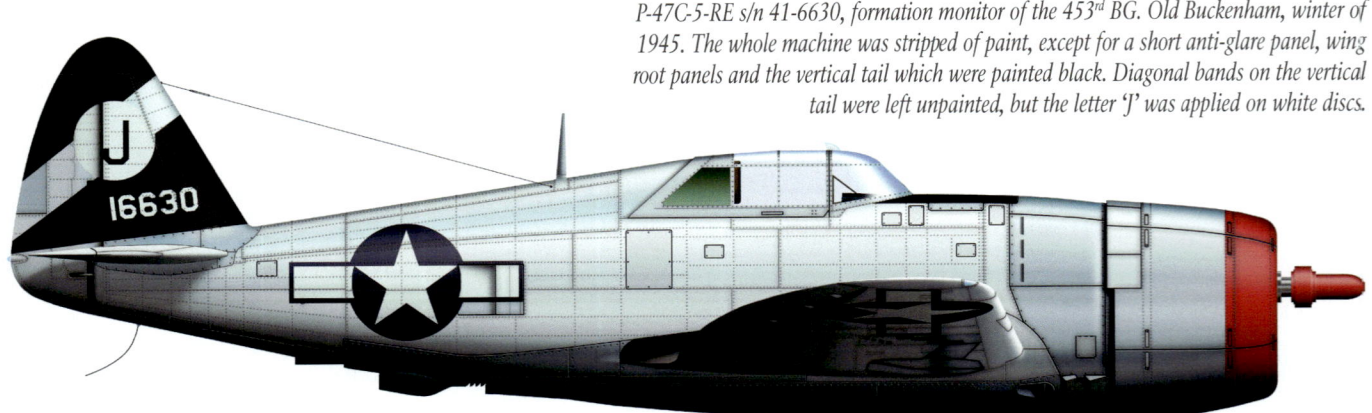

P-47D-2-RE s/n 42-8372 Piccadilly Pete, ffrom the 14th Combat Bombardment Wing's Headquarter Flight. Previously with the 66th Fighter Wing's Headquarter Flight, this Jug was used as a personal plane by Brig General Murray C Woodbury. After a transfer to the 14th CBW, the Piccadilly Pete was striped out of its camouflage except Woodbury's personal badge retained with Olive Drab outline and engine cowling's mosaic. The plane was used as formation monitor at Sta.115 / Shipdham.

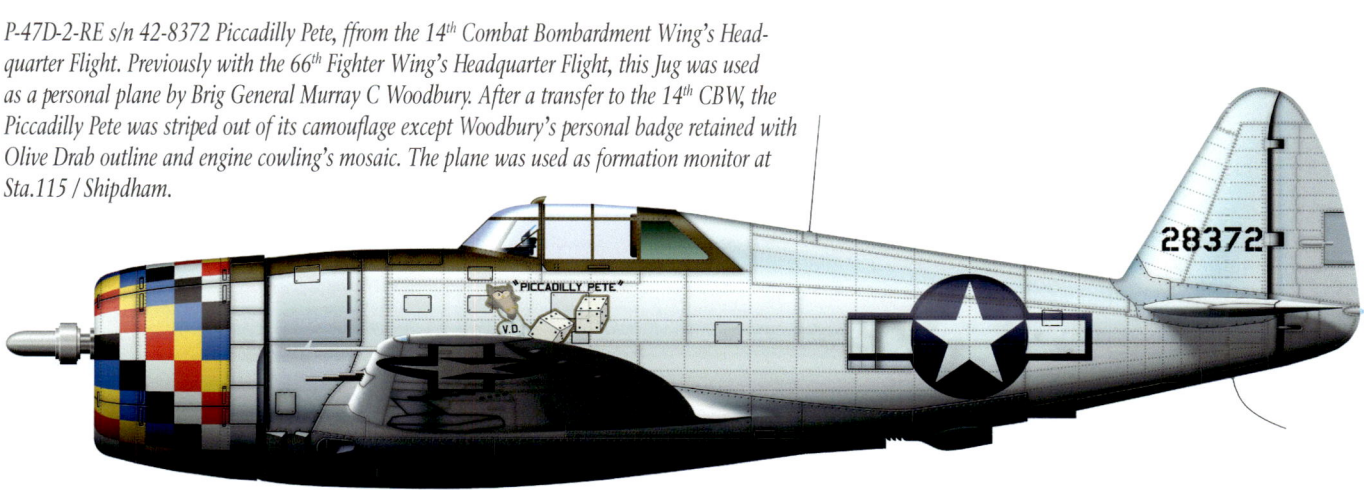

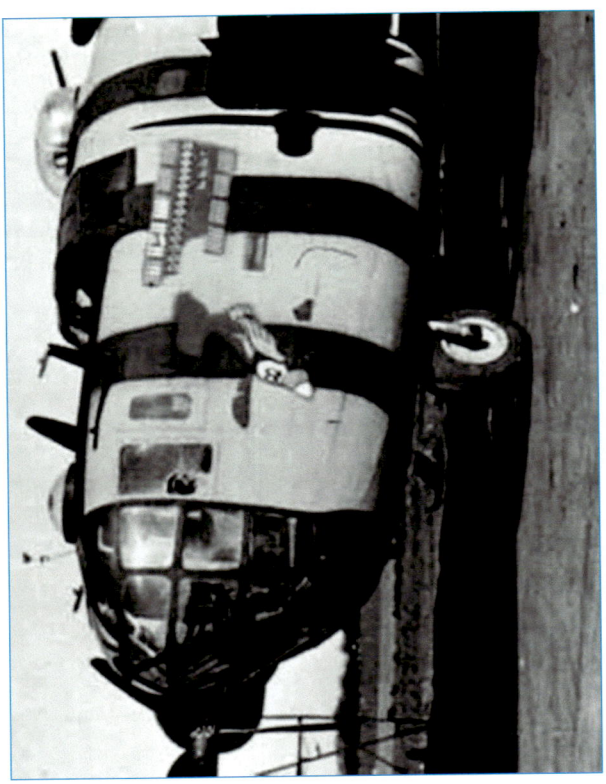

Left: Lemon Drop in its original colours, September 1943.

Right, below, and on opposite page: B-24D-1-CO s/n 41-23699 Lemon Drop assembly ship of the 44th BG. Shipdham, February 1944. One of nine original aircraft that the 68th BS / 44th BG had brought to the UK. Initially, marked as P, the aircraft was changed to WQ•N in November 1943.

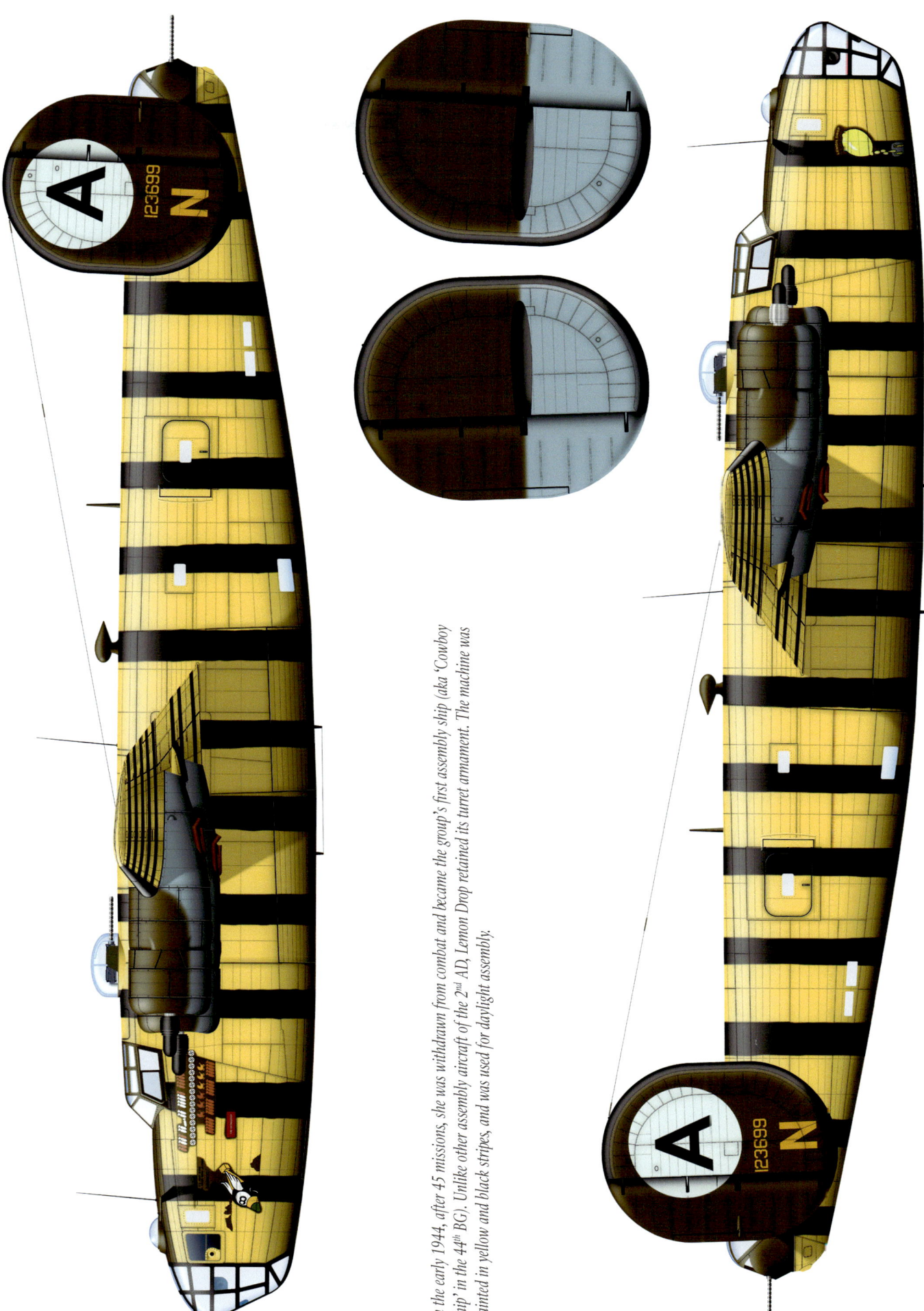

In the early 1944, after 45 missions, she was withdrawn from combat and became the group's first assembly ship (aka 'Cowboy Ship' in the 44th BG). Unlike other assembly aircraft of the 2nd AD, Lemon Drop retained its turret armament. The machine was painted in yellow and black stripes, and was used for daylight assembly.

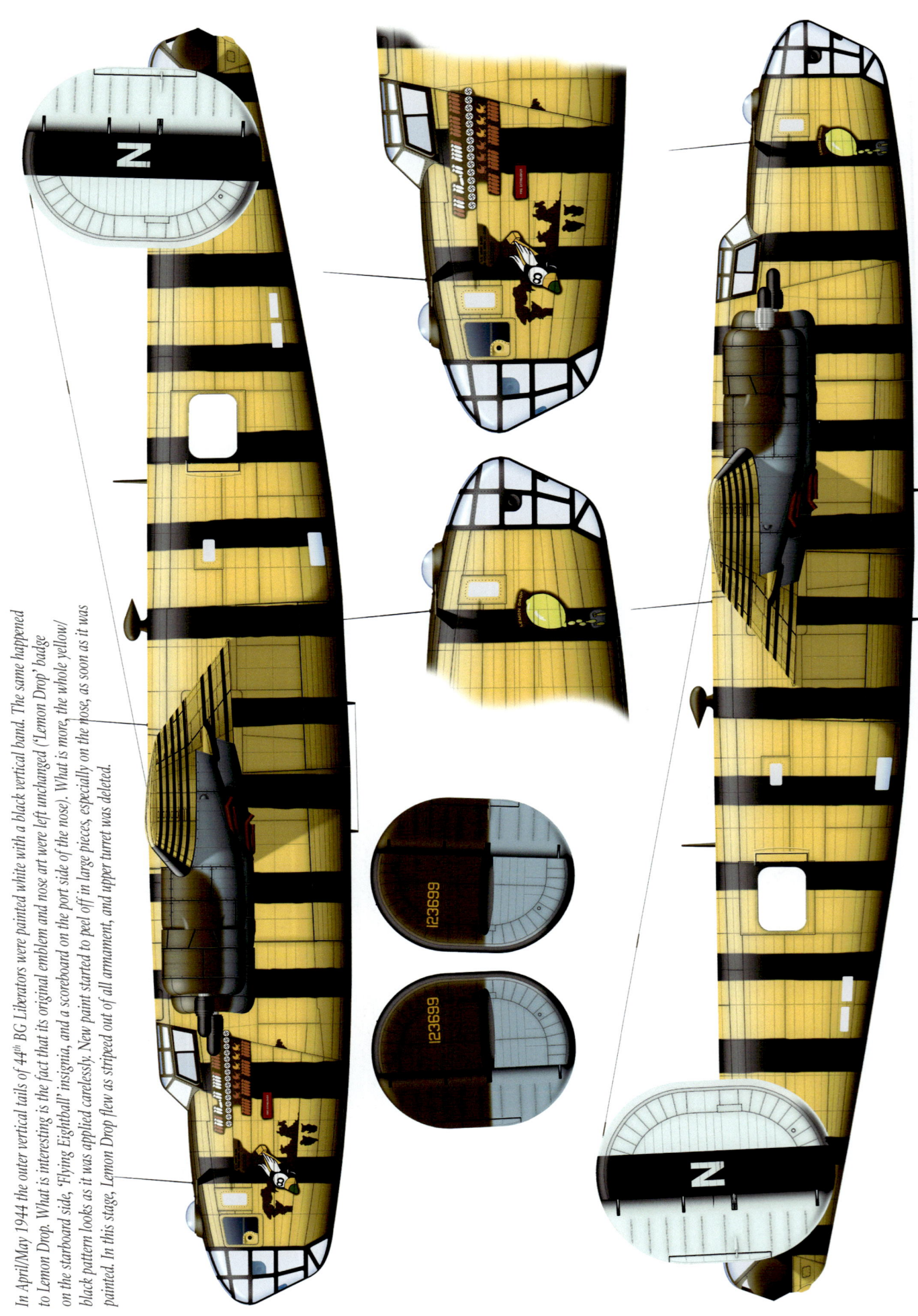

In April/May 1944 the outer vertical tails of 44th BG Liberators were painted white with a black vertical band. The same happened to Lemon Drop. What is interesting is the fact that its original emblem and nose art were left unchanged ('Lemon Drop' badge on the starboard side, 'Flying Eightball' insignia, and a scoreboard on the port side of the nose). What is more, the whole yellow/black pattern looks as it was applied carelessly. New paint started to peel off in large pieces, especially on the nose, as soon as it was painted. In this stage, Lemon Drop flew as stripped out of all armament, and upper turret was deleted.

Top and Above: B-24D-1-CO s/n 41-23699 'Lemon Drop', assembly ship of the 44th BG. Shipdham, February 1944.
Below: 'Lemon Drop' in its original colours, September 1943.

B-24H-5-CF s/n 41-29208 Shoo Shoo Baby, assembly ship of the 44th BG. Shipdham, April 1944.

B-24H-5-CF s/n 41-29208 Shoo Shoo Baby, assembly ship of the 44th BG, Shipdham, April 1944. Originally Shoo Shoo Baby was assigned to the 712th BS / 448th BG where it was marked Triangle/G; it undertook only one mission, on 22nd December 1943. Transferred to the 66th BS / 44th BG, the aircraft performed 19 missions marked as QK●Z+ until March 1944 when it was withdrawn and converted for daybreak assembly missions. Consequently all its turrets were removed, a 'glasshouse' on the nose incorporating a Bell power boost unit and a light installation for pre-dawn forming were added. Because Shoo Shoo Baby carried out its missions before morning twilight it retained its original camouflage of Olive Drab / Neutral Grey because in the dark nobody would even notice an extravagant paint scheme. The only changes in the paint of this aircraft were near the converted nose and the faired-over dismantled top turret. Shoo Shoo Baby returned to the USA on 7th March 1945.

91

P-47C-5-RE s/n 41-6618, the formation monitor of the 44th BG pictured during job from Liberator's left waist gunner's window. Note early stage of markings.

Right: The same plane but with vertical tail painted white. Damaged after landing accident at Shipdam on 25 October 1944 and replaced in it's tasks by Thunderbolt s/n 42-7865.

Above: P-47D-1-RE s/n 42-7865, together with Norseman of the 44th BG. Shipdham, late summer 1944.

P-47D-1-RE s/n 42-7865, formation monitor of the 44th BG. Shipdham, December 1944. The machine is in standard paintwork of Olive Drab / Neutral Grey, except for the natural-metal canopy frames. The vertical tail is painted white with a black vertical band, the colours of 'The Flying Eighthballs'. Note that the aircraft lacks its armament, gunsight and armored glass panel. Invasion stripes are on the lower fuselage surfaces only.

93

P-47D-11-RE, s/n 42-75517 LuLu, formation monitor of the 492ⁿᵈ BG. North Pickenham, August 1944. This aircraft had a short career as a monitor. The machine undertook the function in July and August 1944, and later was transferred to the 466ᵗʰ BG at Attlebridge for the same duties. In the background the B-24D, s/n 42-40743 Zebra a formation assembly aircraft of the 492ⁿᵈ BG, and other utility planes are visible. The aircraft has no armament or gunsight and invasion stripes are on the lower surfaces only.

As an assembly aircraft Zebra retained its Olive Drab / Neutral Grey camouflage with only a few modifications, e.g. Neutral Grey was left only on the undersurfaces of the wings and engines. In other places, the bottom of the fuselage, outer wings, and horizontal tails, a new coat of Olive Drab was applied to create contrast and a background for wide white stripes. The outer parts of the white vertical tail had black diagonal stripes. The squadron's code letters were painted in insignia Blue. Zebra retained its original scoreboard painted on the cockpit's armoured plate. No information is available as to whether Zebra was transferred to another group or remained at North Pickenham when the 492nd BG was disbanded on 7th August 1944. The aircraft was salvaged on the 20th March 1945 in England.

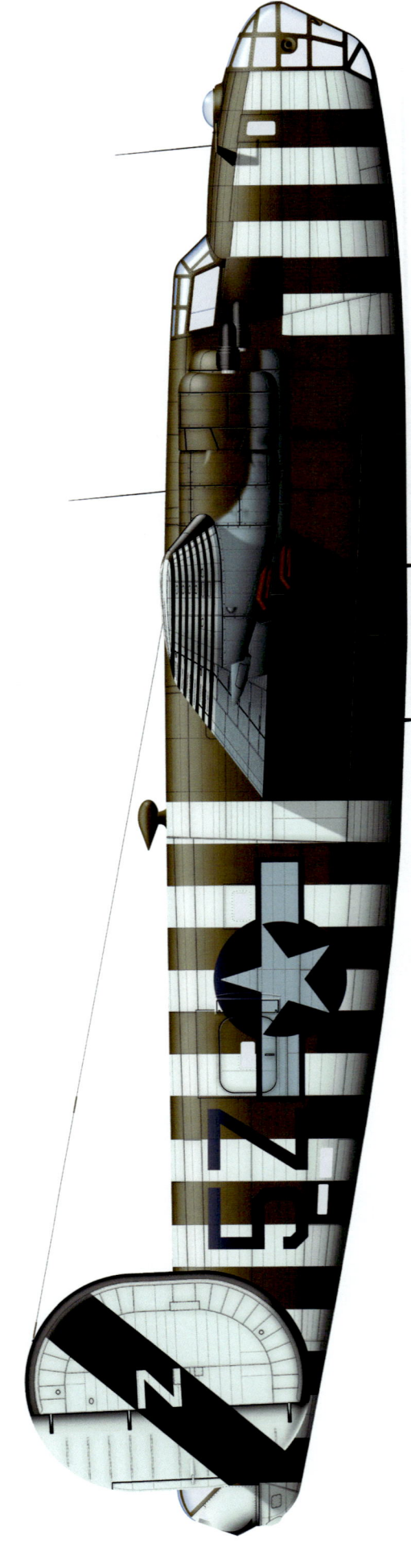

B-24D-95-CO s/n 42-40743 Zebra, assembly ship of the 492nd BG. North Pickenham, May 1944. Before Zebra was sent to become an assembly aircraft of the 492nd BG on 15th May 1944, it was used by the 567th BS / 389th BG's crews. Marked as HP●O – (see photo, page 22), the aircraft performed 56 combat missions, including a famous low-level attack on Ploiesti Oil Refinery complex on 1st August 1943.

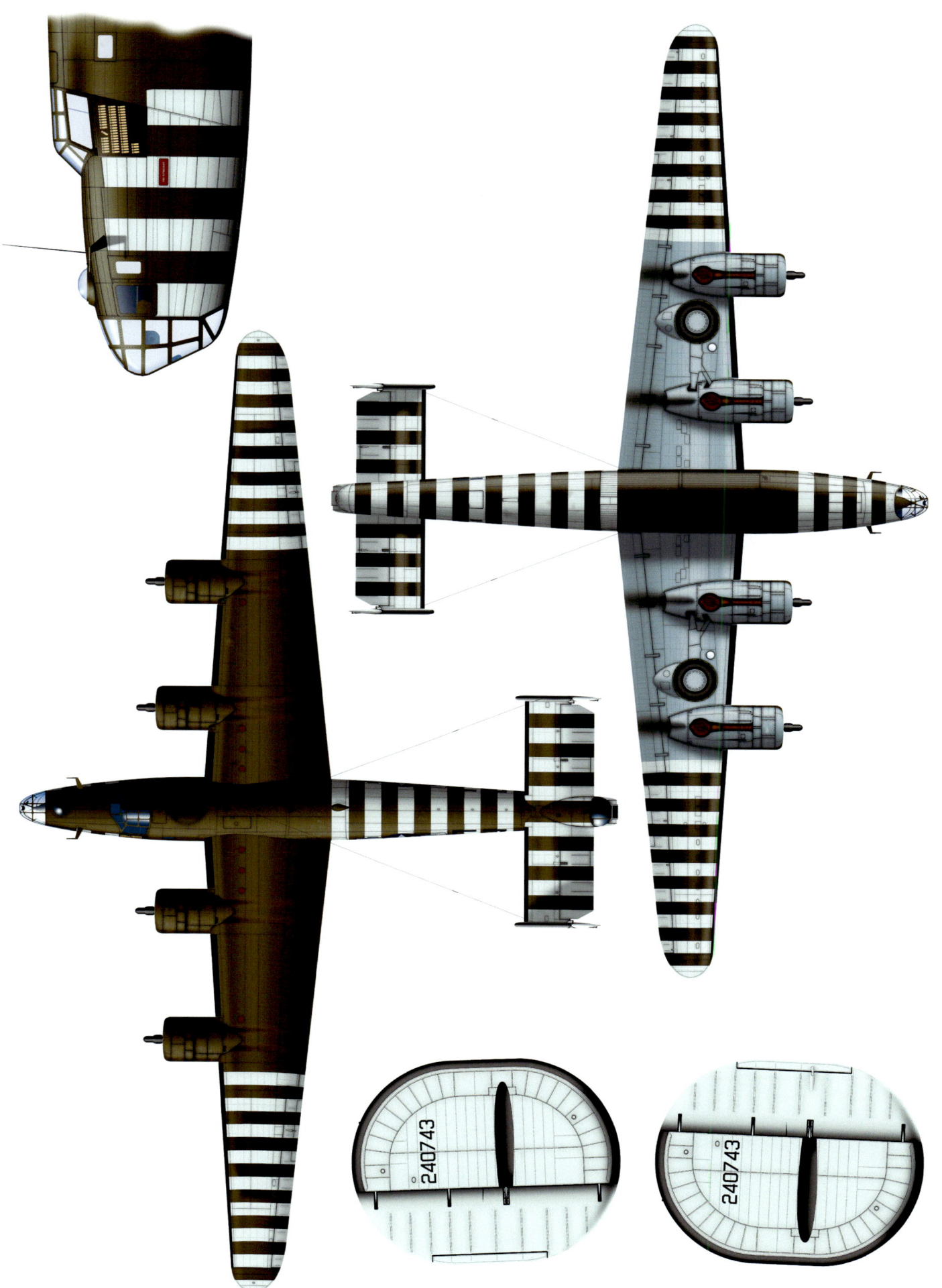

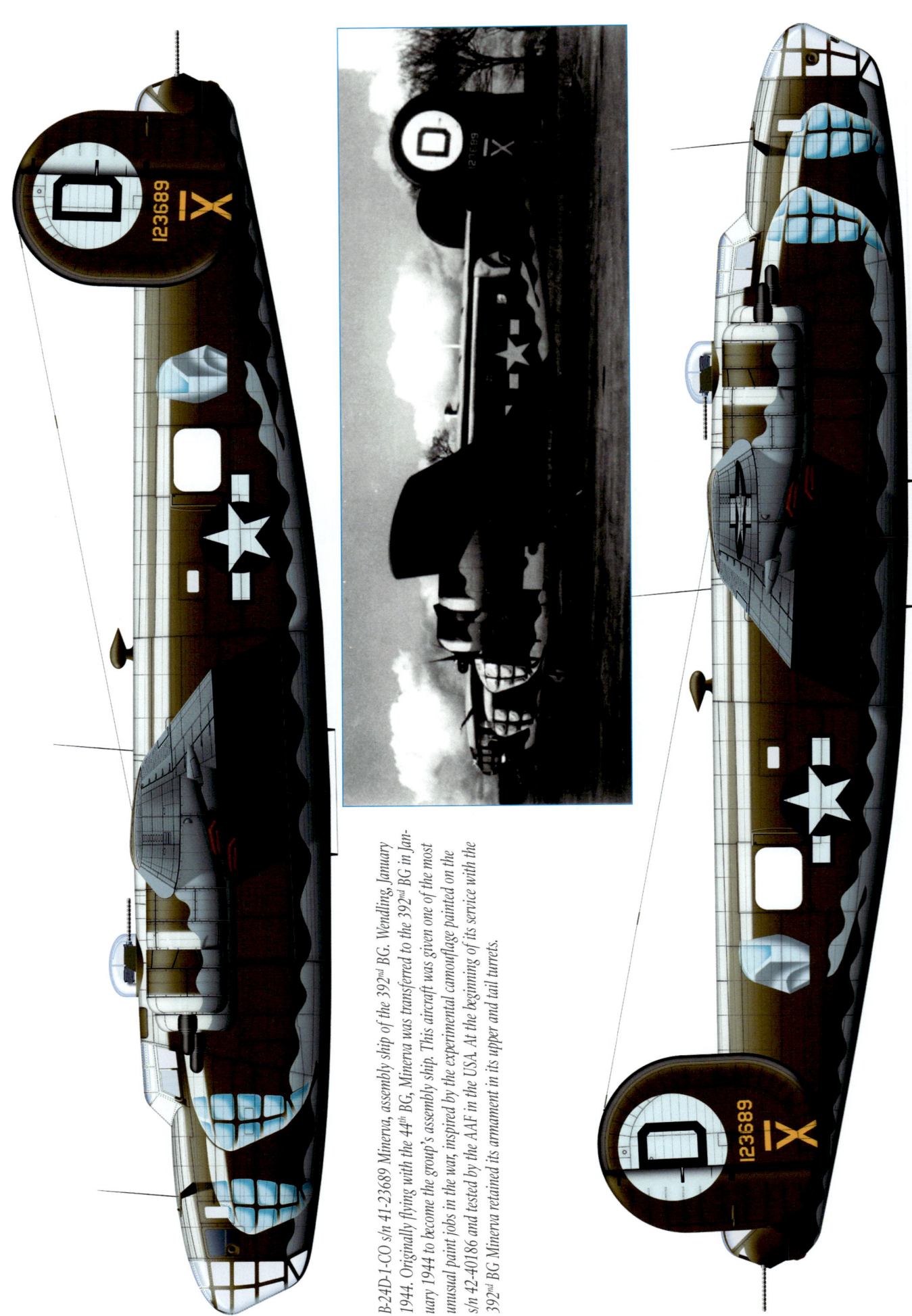

B-24D-1-CO s/n 41-23689 Minerva, assembly ship of the 392nd BG. Wendling, January 1944. Originally flying with the 44th BG, Minerva was transferred to the 392nd BG in January 1944 to become the group's assembly ship. This aircraft was given one of the most unusual paint jobs in the war, inspired by the experimental camouflage painted on the s/n 42-40186 and tested by the AAF in the USA. At the beginning of its service with the 392nd BG Minerva retained its armament in its upper and tail turrets.

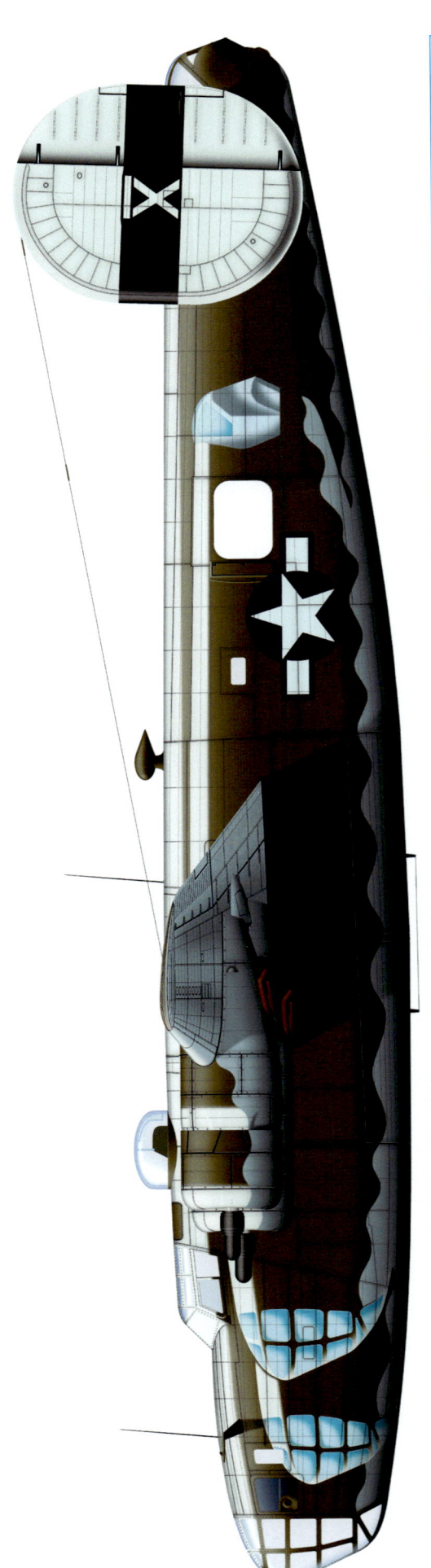

In April 1944 the paintwork on the vertical tails of Minerva was changed. The outer parts of the tail were painted white and given a black horizontal stripe. At the time, the aircraft no longer had its armament. Note that Natural Grey on the undersurfaces was applied with a wavy demarcation style over the wing and horizontal tail leading edges. It was severely damaged in a non-combat mishap sometime in 1944, but was officially salvaged by the 392nd BG on 30 October 1944, and then apparently passed around between several bomb groups. Towards the end of its long career, in April 1945, Minerva carried 52 soldiers with their equipment in an experimental 10-hour flight to determine the feasibility of using bombers to airlift ground personnel home after end of the war in Europe.

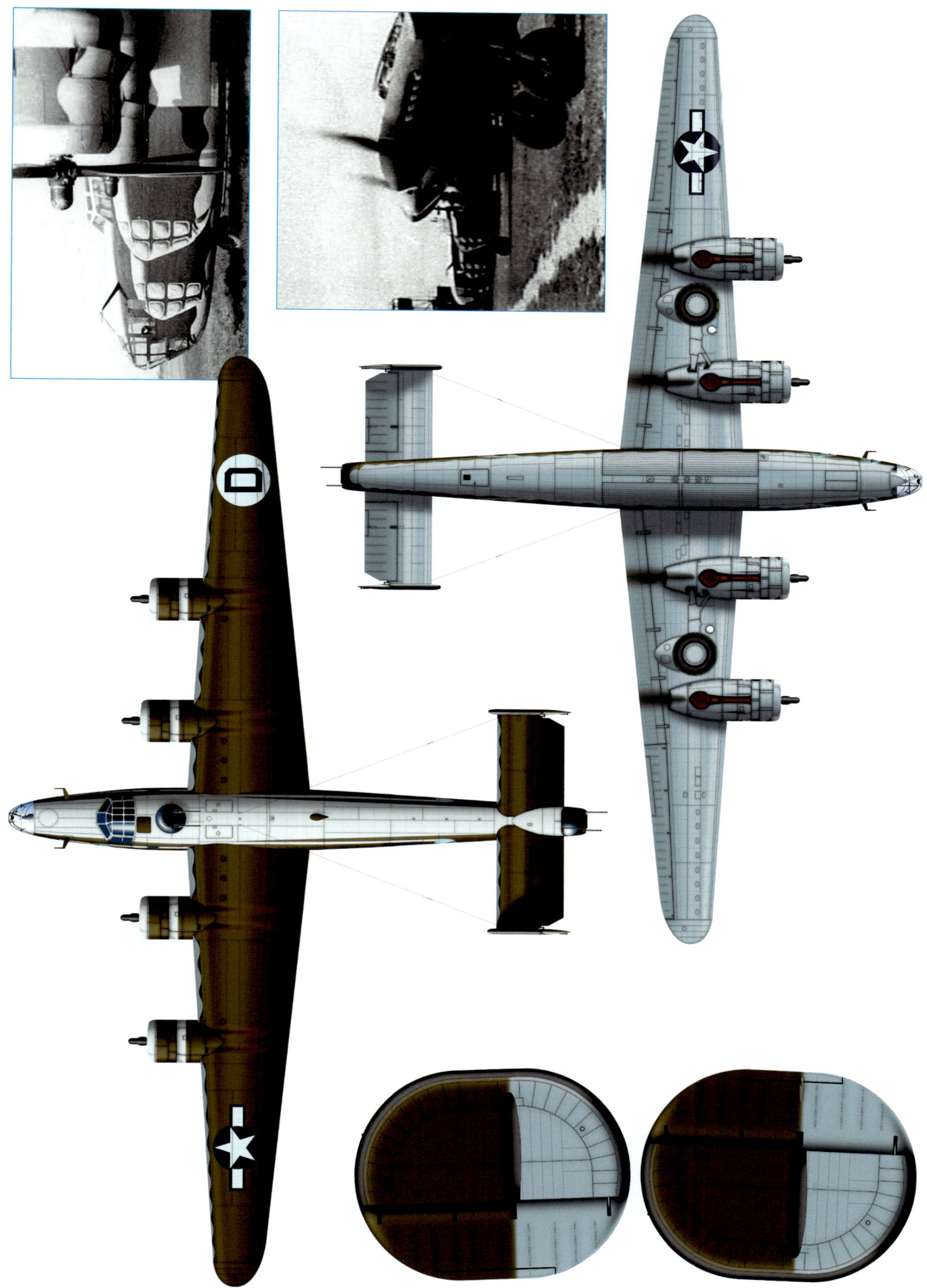

P-47 D-11-RE s/n 42-75434, a formation monitor of the 392nd BG. Former ex – 61st FS / 56th FG HV-C Slugger expirienced with Category 3 damage during take-off accdent at Halesworth, with Lt Norman E Brooks at controls on 1st January 1944. After repair declared as war-weary, and assigned for non-combat duties with 392nd BG. Damaged by Lorin L Johnson on 28th April 1945 due to landing accident at Wendling.

B-24D-90-CO s/n 42-40722 *The Little Gramper*, assembly ship of the 491st BG, Medfield, June 1944.

B-24D-90-CO s/n 42-40722 The Little Gramper, assembly ship of the 491st BG, Medfield, June 1944. Originally the aircraft served with the 567th BS / 389th BG, in which as B – it took part in the 'Tidal Wave' operation (the attack on the Romanian Ploiesti Oil Refinery complex). Next the aircraft was part of the 566th BS / 389th BG, and flew as B+ and then RR●B+. In general the aircraft carried out 52 combat sorties with 'The Sky Scorpions' until May 1944. On 15th May 1944 the aircraft was transfered to the 491st BG where it was lightened by removing the armament and unimportant equipment. The aircraft was painted deep yellow with red polka dots and designated to become an assembly aircraft. The Little Gramper in its new role as assembly ship served for only two months, and was replaced by one of the group's war-weary B-24Js, Rage In Heaven.

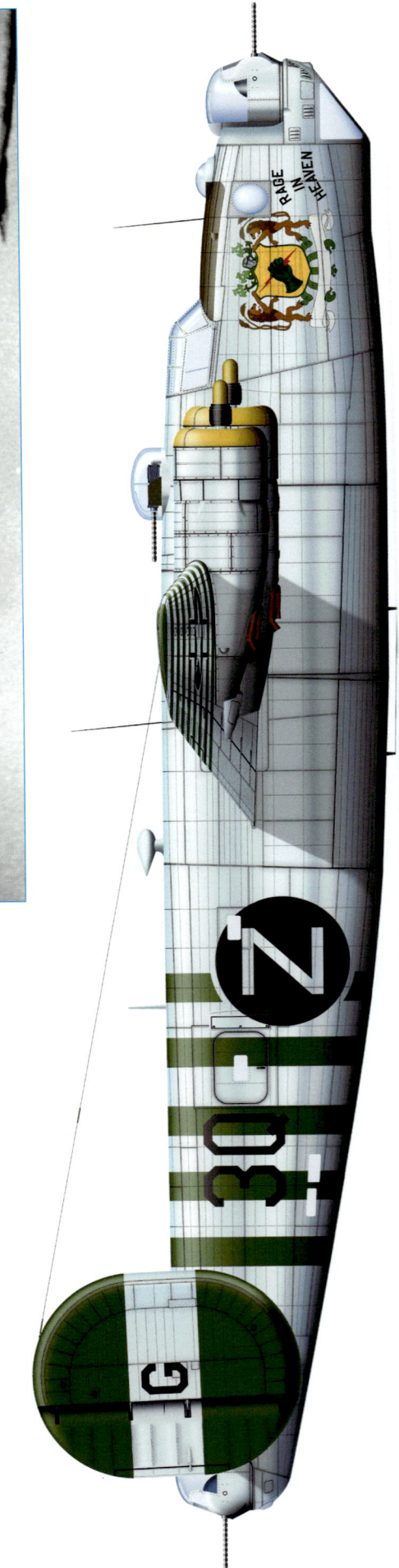

B-24J-150-CO s/n 44-40165 *Rage In Heaven*, assembly ship of the 491st BG. North Pickenham, September 1944. When the 95th CBW was disbanded in August 1944, the 491st BG moved over to North Pickenham to replace the 492nd BG in the 14th CBW. Besides all those organizational changes, a very war-weary *Little Gramper* was abandoned at Metfield. *Rage In Heaven* was assigned as the group's new formation assembly aircraft. When with the 852nd BS the aircraft performed three dozen combat missions as 3Q●G. As an assembly aircraft *Rage In Heaven* received green zebra stripes around the original nose art and a scoreboard. The outer parts of the vertical tails were painted green with horizontal bands left unpainted. Note that the No.1 engine cowling had been taken from another Liberator. *Rage In Heaven* crashed, exploded and burnt on 5th January 1945 near Swaffham after taking off in a snowstorm to lead the assembly of the group. The second B-24 crashed a few minutes later because of icy conditions. Eventually, the mission was cancelled.

B-24J-150-CO s/n 44-40165 *Rage In Heaven*, assembly ship of the 491st BG. North Pickenham, September 1944.

B-24J-145-CO s/n 44-40101 *Tubarão, assembly ship of the 491st BG. North Pickenham, January 1945.*

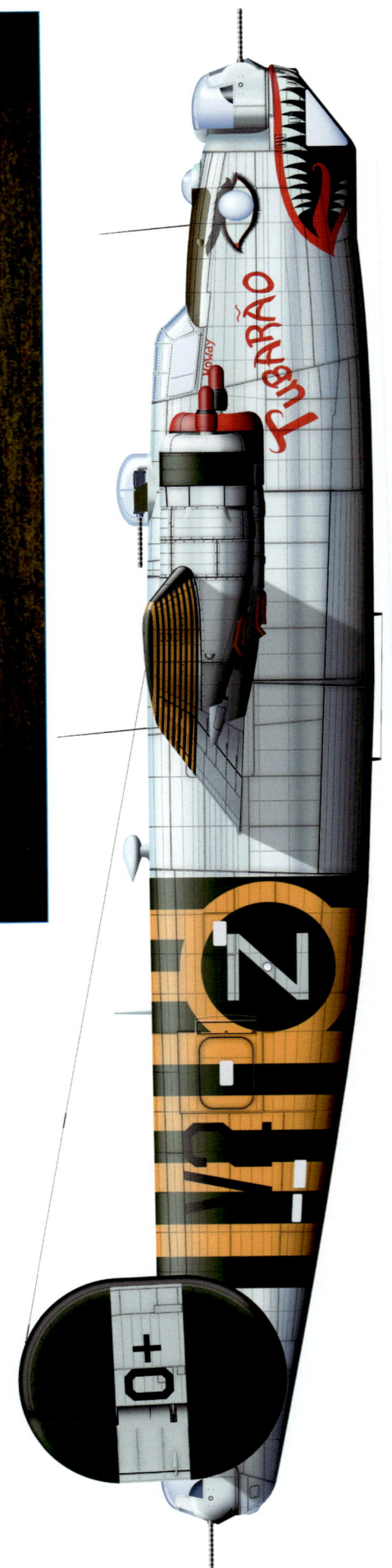

B-24J-145-CO s/n 44-40101 Tubarão, assembly ship of the 491st BG. North Pickenham, January 1945. After Rage In Heaven crashed, a twenty-mission veteran of the 491st BG, Tubarão was given the job. The aircraft was painted in now-familiar zebra treatment, this time in green and yellow. Tubarão ('shark' in Portuguese), formerly a 855th BS machine, had originally been adorned with a huge shark's mouth, which was retained, so that the finished product was a rather curious hybrid of fish in front and zebra behind. Outer parts of the vertical tail were painted green with a white horizontal band. Like Rage In Heaven, Tubarão kept its defensive armament. Note that the front port side bomb bay doors were probably taken from another Liberator. This aircraft served as the formation aircraft until the end of combat operations.

At the turn of March and April 1945 the 491st BG's Liberators started to use former 492nd BG markings, outer parts of vertical tails were silver or white with black diagonal stripe. On this page you can see Tubarão during last months of the war.

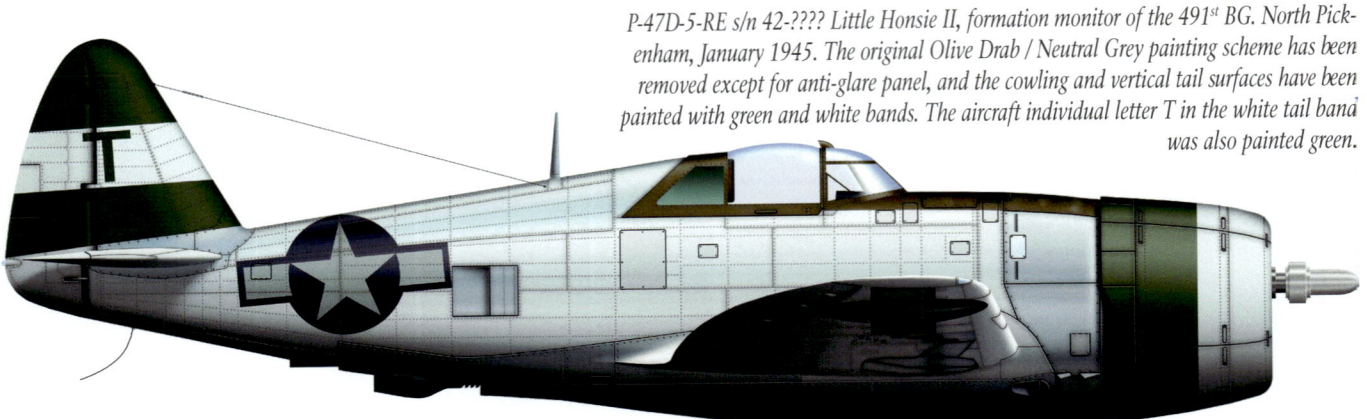

P-47D-5-RE s/n 42-???? Little Honsie II, formation monitor of the 491st BG. North Pickenham, January 1945. The original Olive Drab / Neutral Grey painting scheme has been removed except for anti-glare panel, and the cowling and vertical tail surfaces have been painted with green and white bands. The aircraft individual letter T in the white tail band was also painted green.

Ball Of Fire was an original 93rd BG plane. Badly damaged in the course of five combat missions during the autumn of 1942, it was removed from combat and used as an air ambulance and for target-towing duties. It does not appear that any distinctive paintwork was applied to this aircraft for some weeks and that the initial modifications were an array of electric lights to give prominence to this aircraft in darkness. The first documented reference to the use of a special aircraft for assembling a formation appears to be that in the records of the 93rd BG, which state that on 30th November 1943, Ball Of Fire was used as a 'rendezvous ship', which means that s/n 41-23667 was the first aircraft to be used as an assembly aircraft. A positive experience with this helper was soon noted by the command of the 2nd Air Division. In late 1943 one of the old 93rd BG Liberators (s/n 41-23683, Jo Jo's Special Delivery) was turned over to the 389th BG at Hethel where, in the first week of 1944, it was used as a 'Zebra Forming Aircraft'. At the same time three B-24 Groups that had recently arrived in the UK were assigned war-weary Liberators from the 93rd BG, suggesting that the assembly ship system had official blessing.

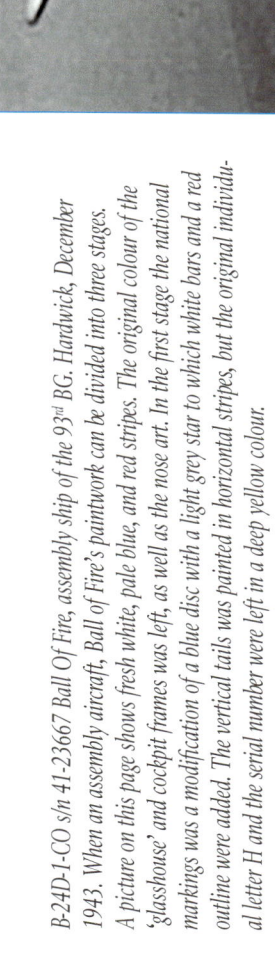

B-24D-1-CO s/n 41-23667 Ball Of Fire, assembly ship of the 93rd BG, Hardwick, December 1943. When an assembly aircraft, Ball of Fire's paintwork can be divided into three stages. A picture on this page shows fresh white, pale blue, and red stripes. The original colour of the 'glasshouse' and cockpit frames was left, as well as the nose art. In the first stage the national markings was a modification of a blue disc with a light grey star to which white bars and a red outline were added. The vertical tails was painted in horizontal stripes, but the original individual letter H and the serial number were left in a deep yellow colour.

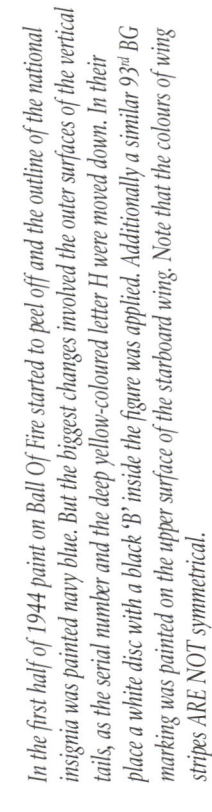
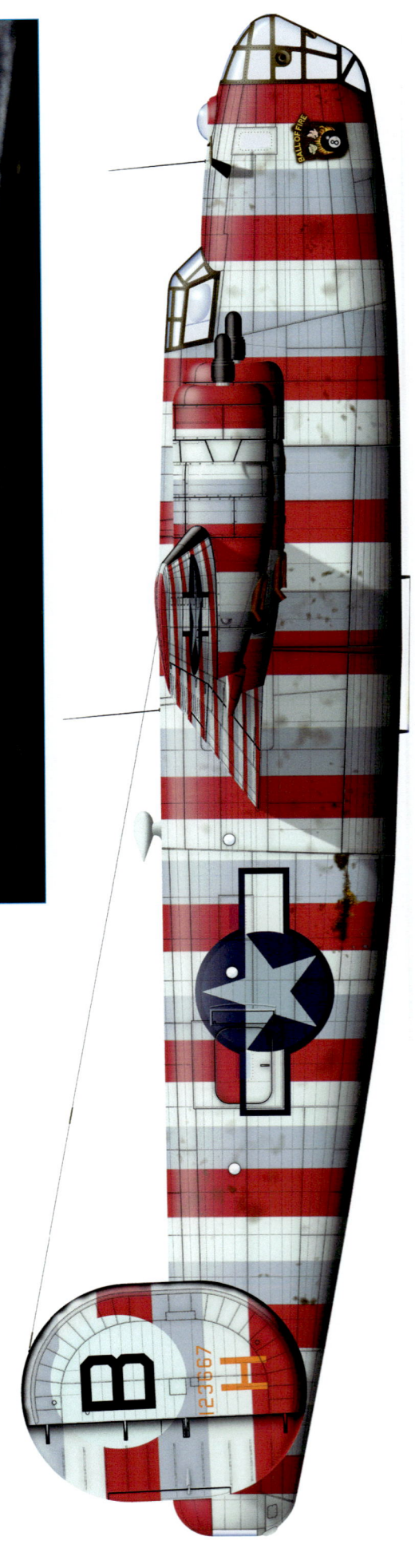

In the first half of 1944 paint on Ball Of Fire started to peel off and the outline of the national insignia was painted navy blue. But the biggest changes involved the outer surfaces of the vertical tails, as the serial number and the deep yellow-coloured letter H were moved down. In their place a white disc with a black 'B' inside the figure was applied. Additionally a similar 93rd BG marking was painted on the upper surface of the starboard wing. Note that the colours of wing stripes ARE NOT symmetrical.

In May 1944 the outer vertical tails of Liberators of the 93rd BG were painted deep yellow with a black vertical band. In this last stage of using Ball Of Fire as an assembly aircraft the outer vertical tail colour was changed to deep yellow. What's most interesting is that the black vertical band was omitted, and the serial number, along with the letter H, changed place again. In September 1944 Ball Of Fire was withdrawn from use, and in May 1945 the aircraft was salvaged and scrapped.

P-47D-?-RE s/n 42-????, probably the formation monitor of the 93rd BG. Hardwick, September 1944. From the information given it is known that the 93rd BG used a P-47 as the formation monitor. However, it was impossible for the authors to find its serial number. We believe that the picture of the 93rd Group's Liberators taken at Orléans in September 1944, shows that aircraft. You can see it in the top right corner of the picture.

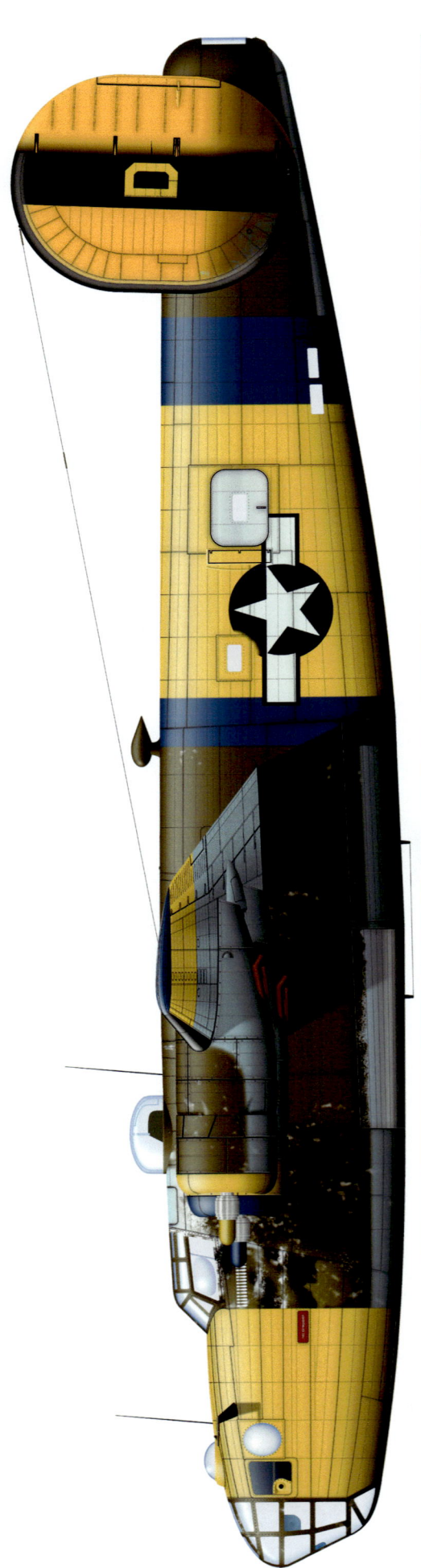

Bear Down just before it was assigned as the formation assembly ship.

B-24D-165-CO s/n 42-72869 Bear Down, assembly ship of the 93rd BG. Hardwick, August 1944. The second assembly aircraft of the 93rd BG was war-weary Bear Down, a veteran of over 45 missions. Although its assembly ship paintwork was not as expressive as Ball Of Fire the aircraft was not difficult to notice! The aircraft had broad yellow bands on the fuselage and outer wings with supplementary blue fuselage bands and wingtips. Note that the front port side bomb bay doors are stripped of paint, probably taken from another Liberator. Bear Down served as the formation aircraft until the end of the war.

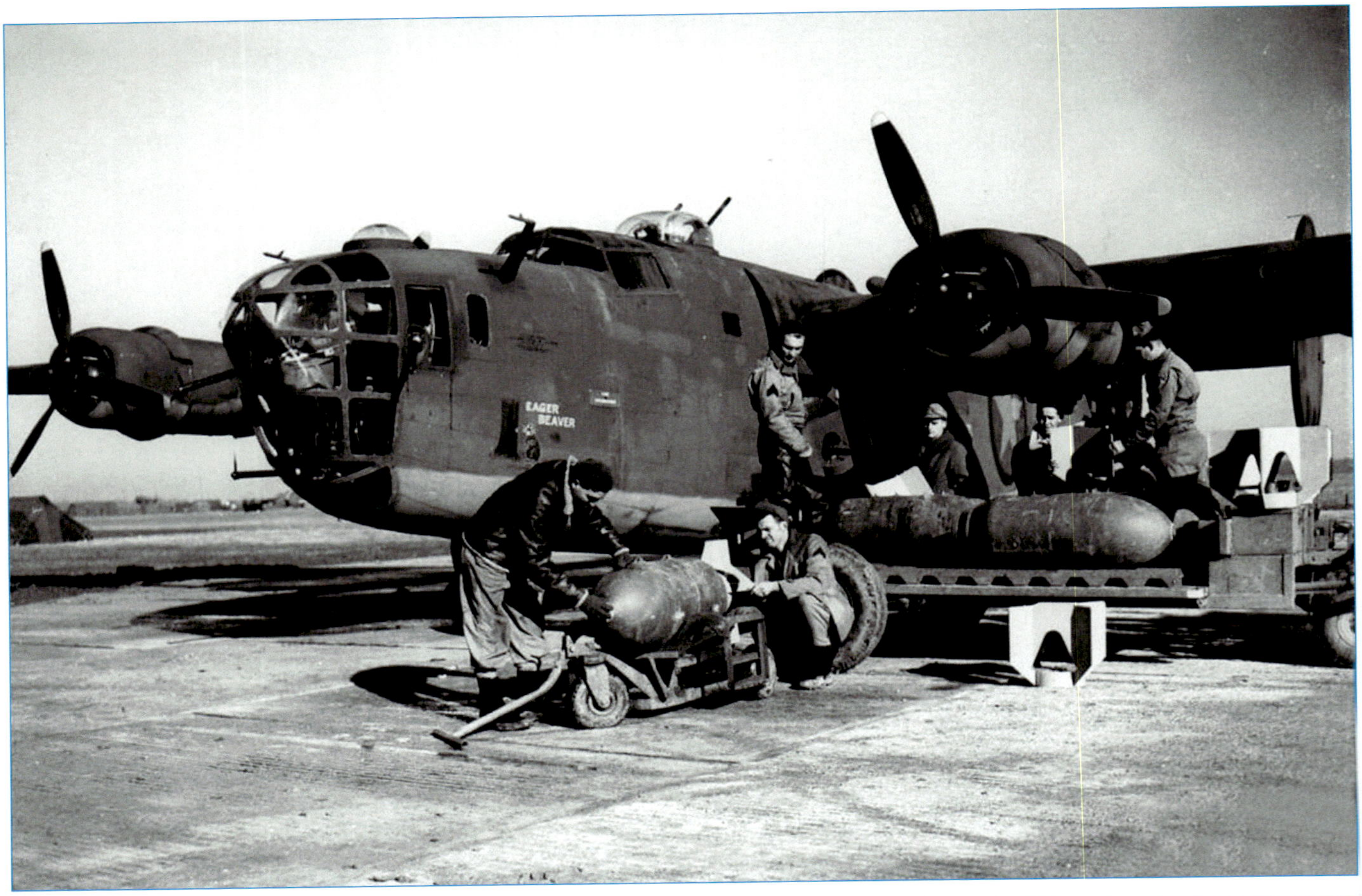
EAGER
BEAVER

EAGER
BEAVER

EAGER
BEAVER

EAGER
BEAVER

EAGER
BEAVER

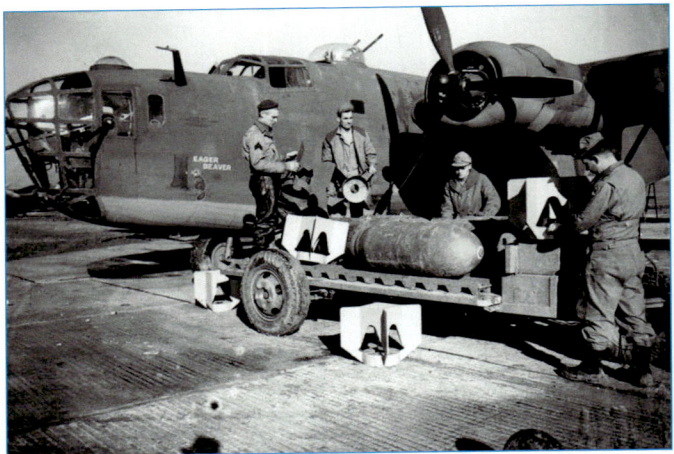

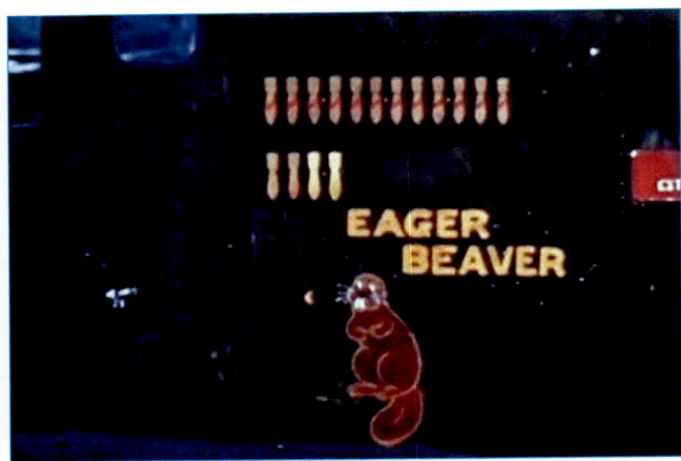

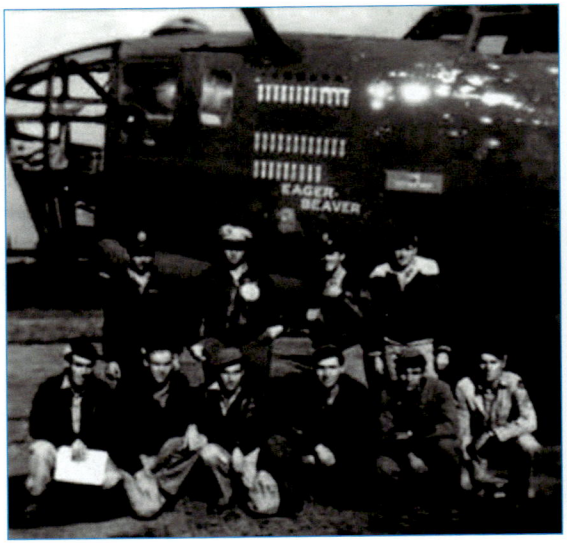

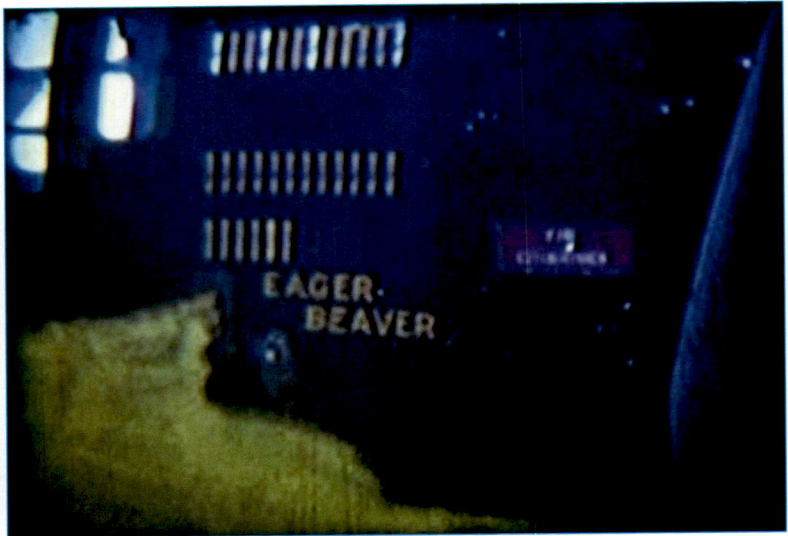

B-24D-1-CO s/n 41-23737 Fearless Freddie, assembly ship of the 446th BG. Bungay, February 1944.

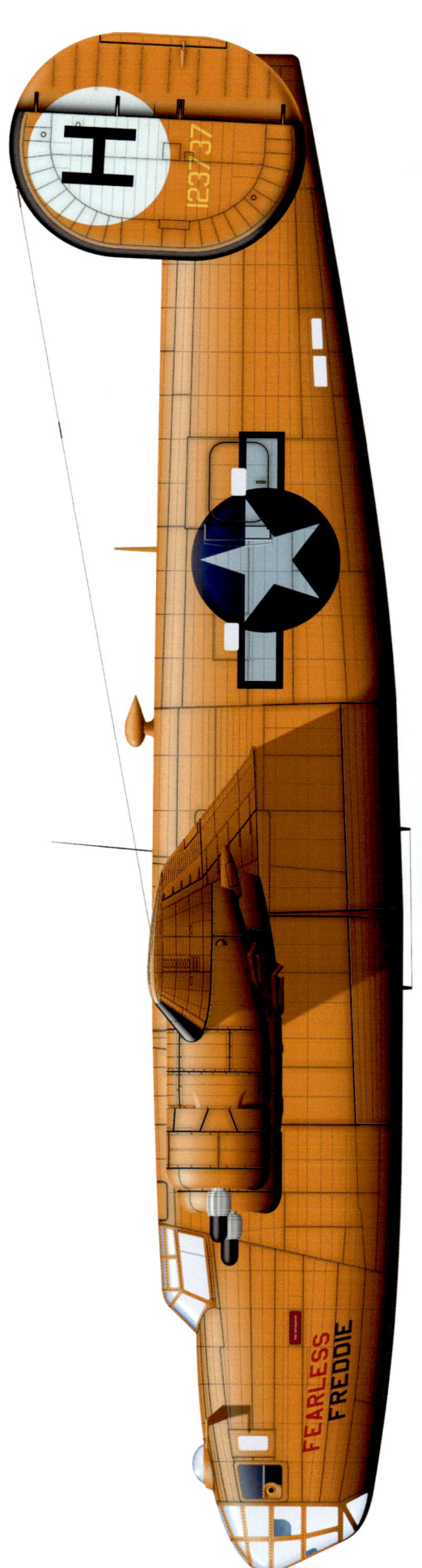
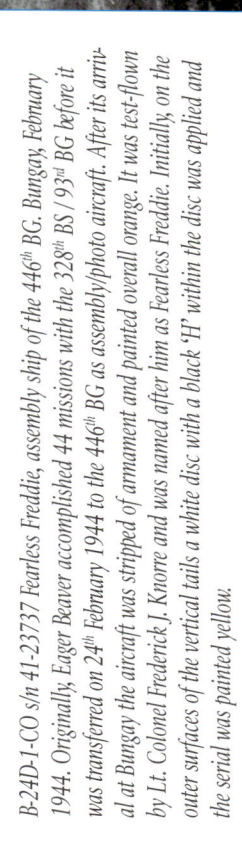
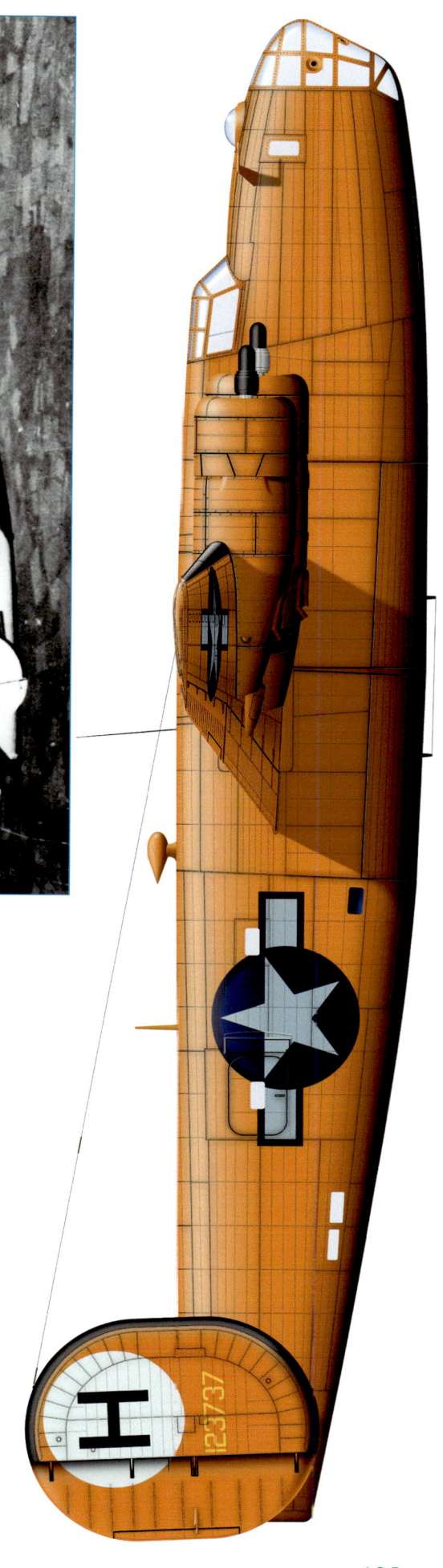

B-24D-1-CO s/n 41-23737 Fearless Freddie, assembly ship of the 446th BG, Bungay, February 1944. Originally, Eager Beaver accomplished 44 missions with the 328th BS / 93rd BG before it was transferred on 24th February 1944 to the 446th BG as assembly/photo aircraft. After its arrival at Bungay the aircraft was stripped of armament and painted overall orange. It was test-flown by Lt. Colonel Frederick J. Knorre and was named after him as Fearless Freddie. Initially, on the outer surfaces of the vertical tails a white disc with a black 'H' within the disc was applied and the serial was painted yellow.

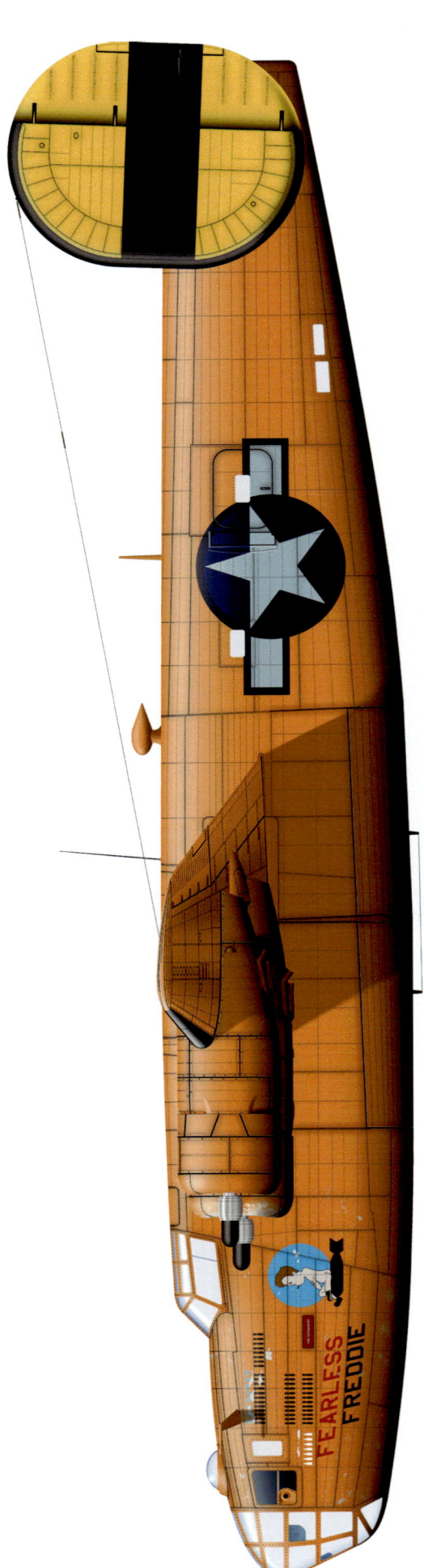

Sometime in the spring of 1944 the nose of the aircraft was given a scoreboard of combat mission from its previous incarnation Eager Beaver. In May 1944, all 446th BG planes had their outer vertical tails painted deep yellow with a black horizontal stripe. Note that the orange paint started to peel and come off, especially on the nose and No.2 engine cowling. In September 1944 Fearless Freddie was replaced by B-24H-1-FO, s/n 42-7654, Fearless Freddie II – ex-Pistol Packin Mamma (salvaged on 29th January 1945 after a crash landing).

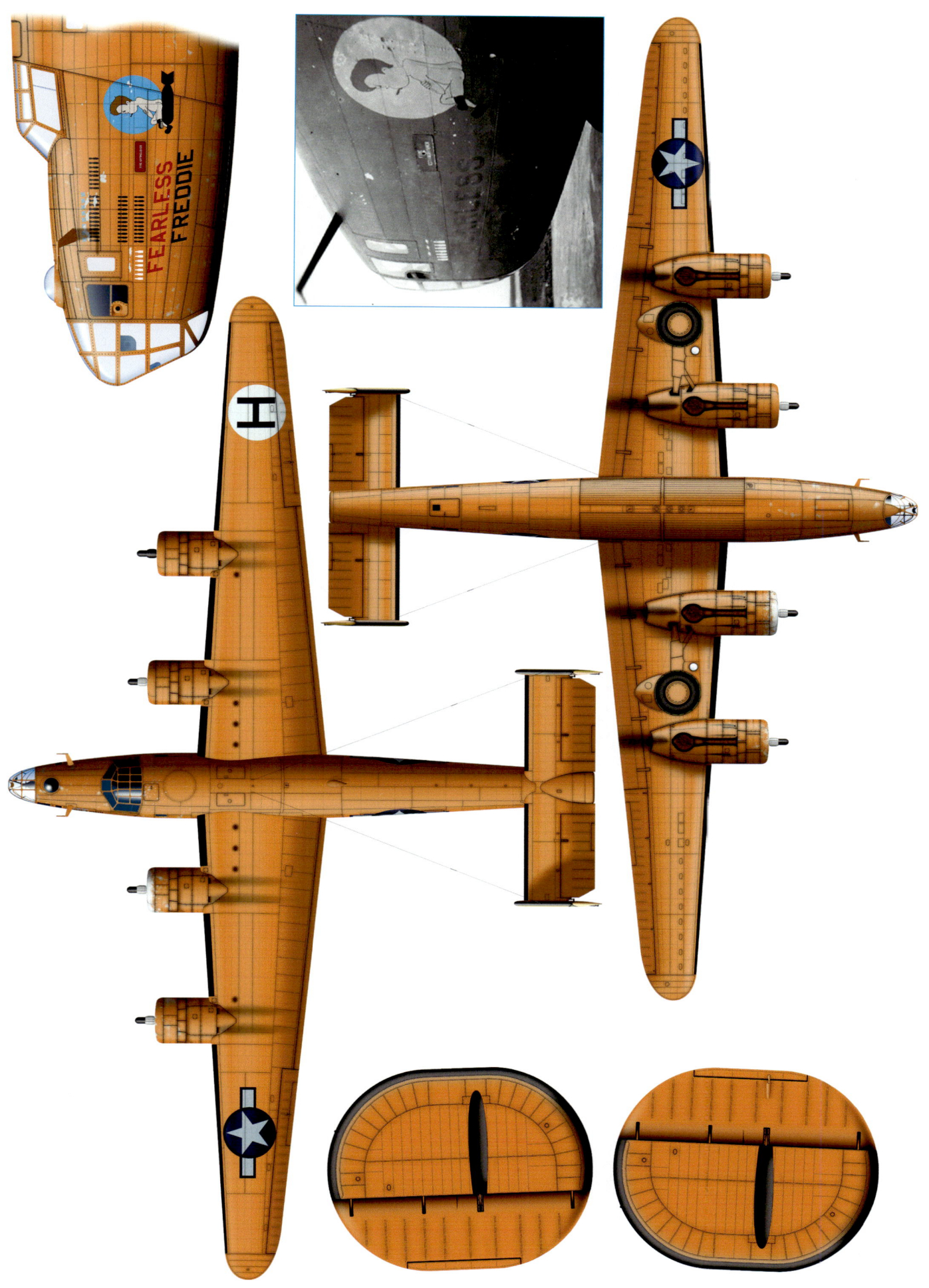

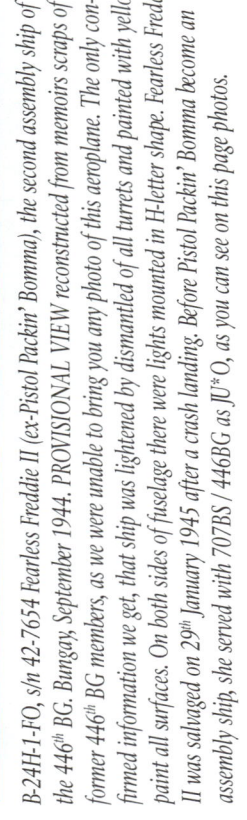

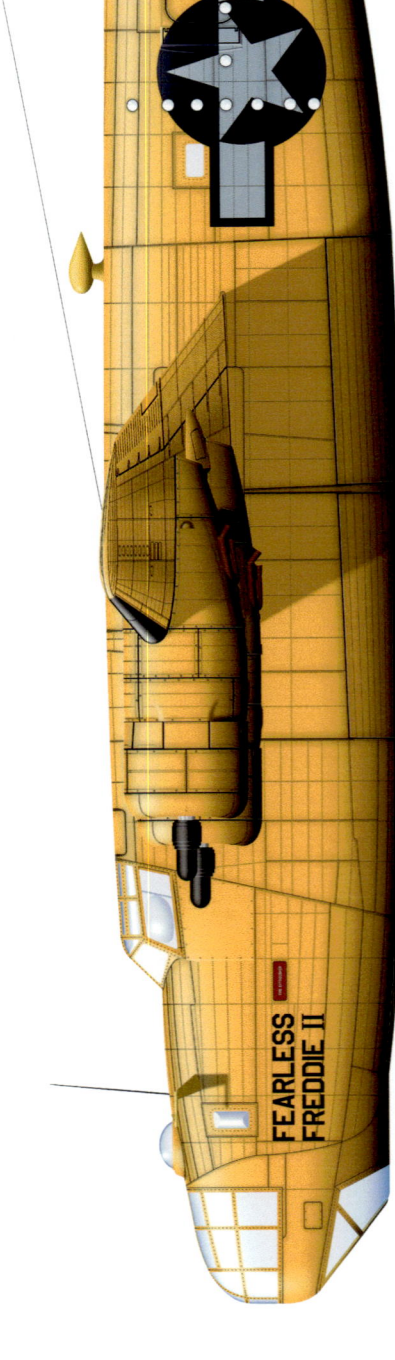

B-24H-1-FO, s/n 42-7654 Fearless Freddie II (ex-Pistol Packin' Bomma), the second assembly ship of the 446th BG, Bungay, September 1944. PROVISIONAL VIEW reconstructed from memoirs scraps of former 446th BG members, as we were unable to bring you any photo of this aeroplane. The only confirmed information we get, that ship was lightened by dismantled of all turrets and painted with yellow paint all surfaces. On both sides of fuselage there were lights mounted in H-letter shape. Fearless Freddie II was salvaged on 29th January 1945 after a crash landing. Before Pistol Packin' Bomma become an assembly ship, she served with 707BS / 446BG as JU∗O, as you can see on this page photos.

*P-47C-5-RE s/n 41-????
The Old Man, formation monitor of the 446th BG. Bungay, August 1944. Just like any other bomb group, the 446th BG had their own disarmed Thunderbolt that was used as the formation monitor. However, beside a few photographs, nothing more is known about this aircraft. We do not even know its serial number. Note the replaced lower panel in the engine cowling painted Neutral Grey, a part that was probably taken from another P-47, and the stars on the main wheel hubs.*

B-24D-5-CO s/n 41-23809 You Cawn't Miss It, assembly ship of the 448th BG. Seething, February 1944. Like most of the original assembly aircraft You Cawn't Miss It had previously served with the 93rd BG, where as Hellsadroppin' II it performed 38 combat sorties. In January 1944, the aircraft was transferred to the 448th BG, disarmed, and painted in black and yellow checkerboard. Initially, the distinctive pattern was restricted to the fuselage, inner and lower parts of the outer vertical tails surfaces. Note the original Hellsadroppin' II scoreboard and row of four positional lights on each side of the rear fuselage.

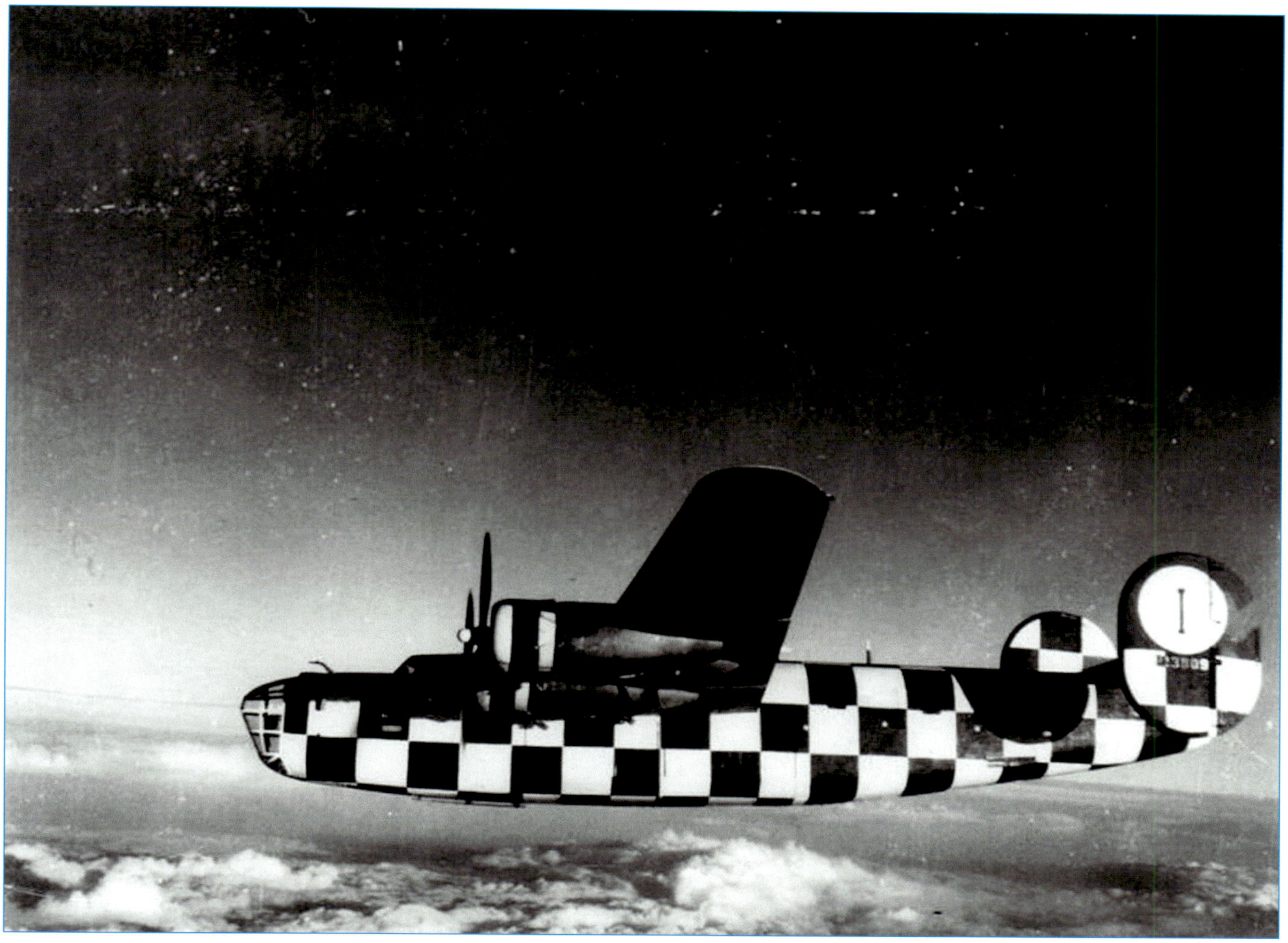
I

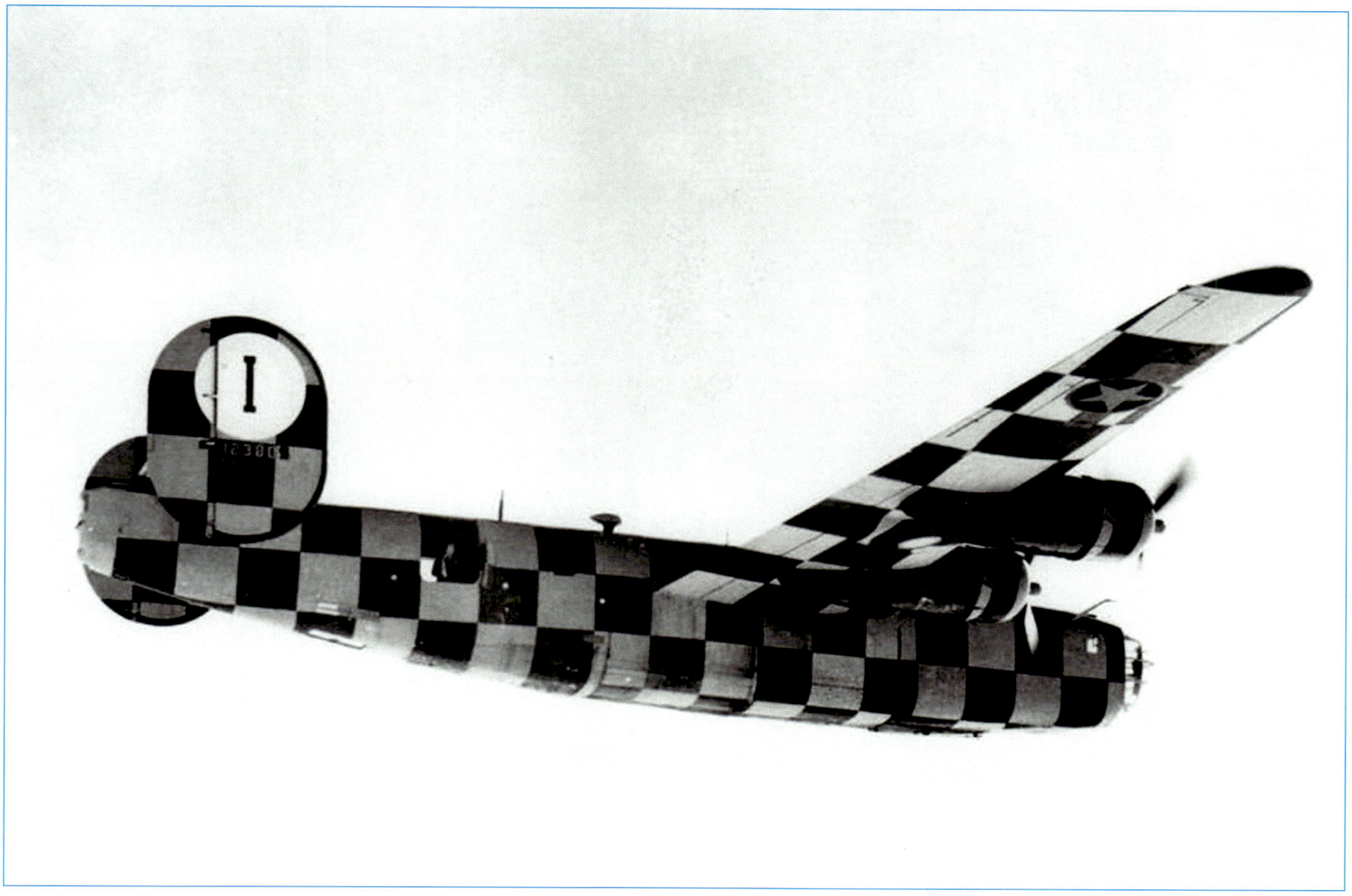
I

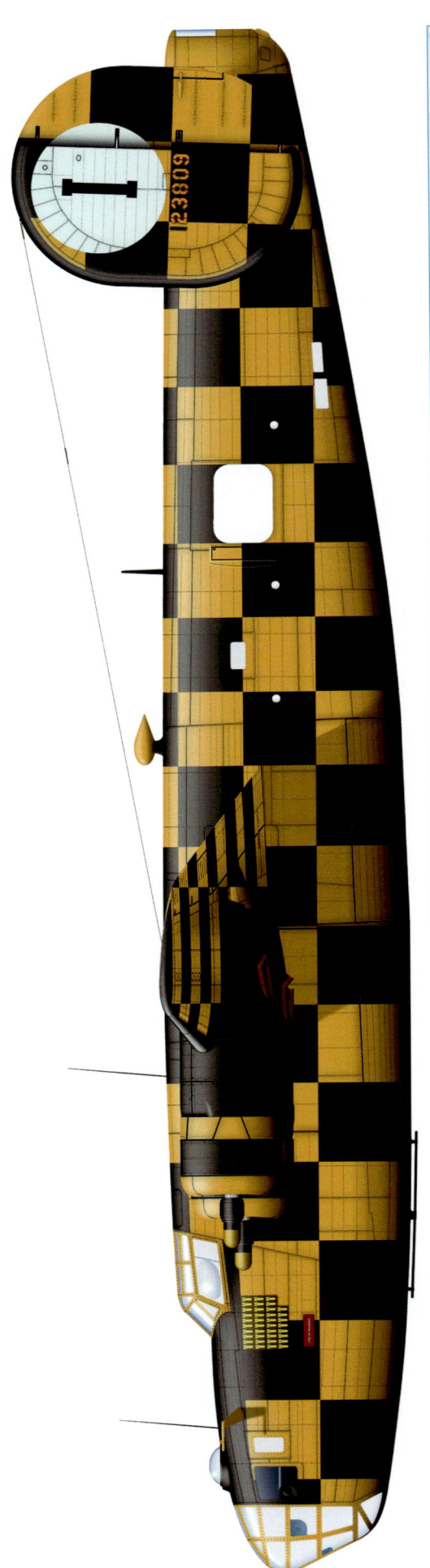

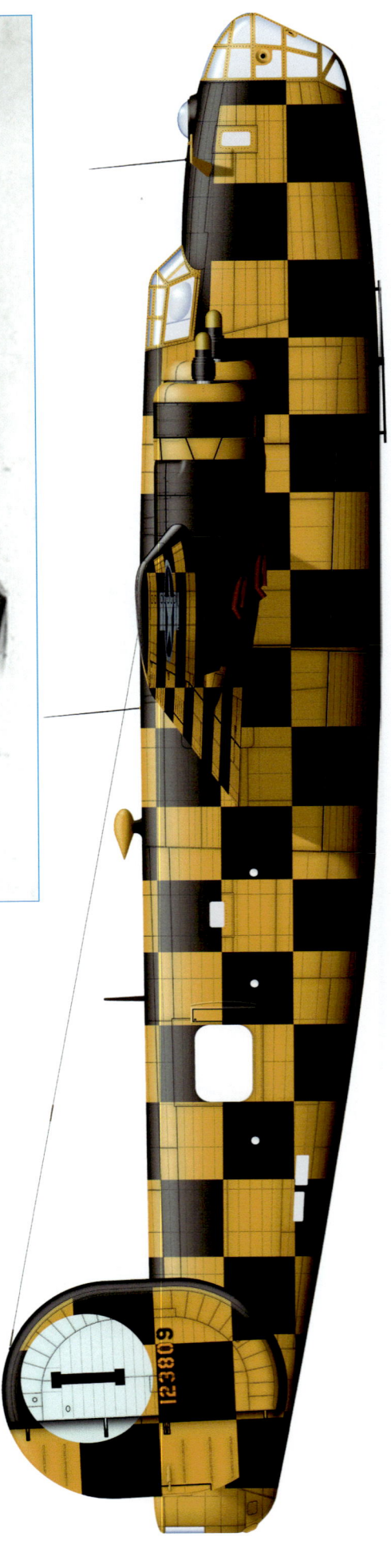

Sometime in the spring of 1944 wing areas were also decorated with yellow and black squares. From this time, You Cawn't Miss It was covered with checkerboard on all surfaces. The last lights in the rows on each side of the fuselage were dismantled for an unknown reason. Due to the deteriorating mechanical condition of the veteran bomber, it was replaced by another B-24 in June 1944.

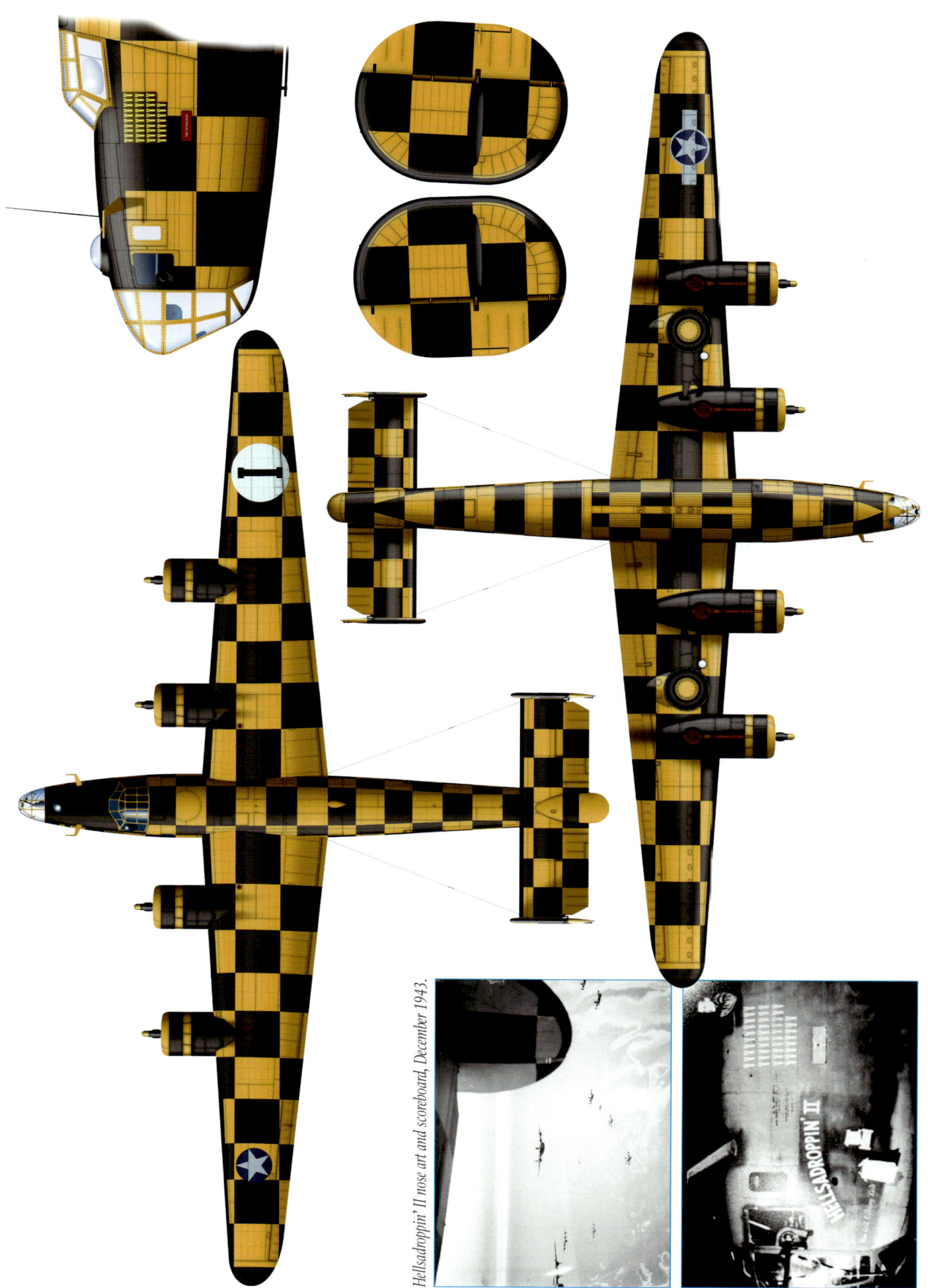

Hellsadroppin' II nose art and scoreboard, December 1943.

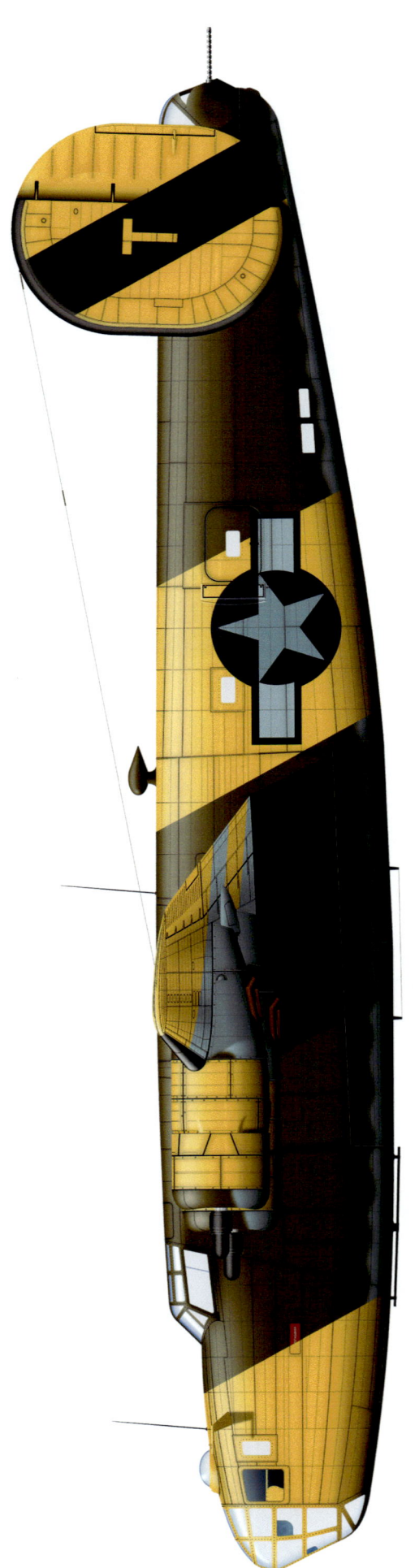

B-24D-20-CF s/n 42-63981 The Striped Ape, assembly ship of the 448th BG. Seething, June 1944. Thanks to Mr Stephen Adams, who bring us above photo, at last we know how The Striped Ape (1st) looks like. The aircraft replaced You Cawn't Miss It in the job of assembly ship in June 1944. The machine was condemned for salvage in February 1945, and replaced by B-24H-15-CF, s/n 41-29489, which was also given the name The Striped Ape. We know, from fragmentary information, that the aircraft retained its Olive Drab / Neutral Grey camouflage, on which yellow diagonal stripes were painted. The plane kept all standard national and group markings.

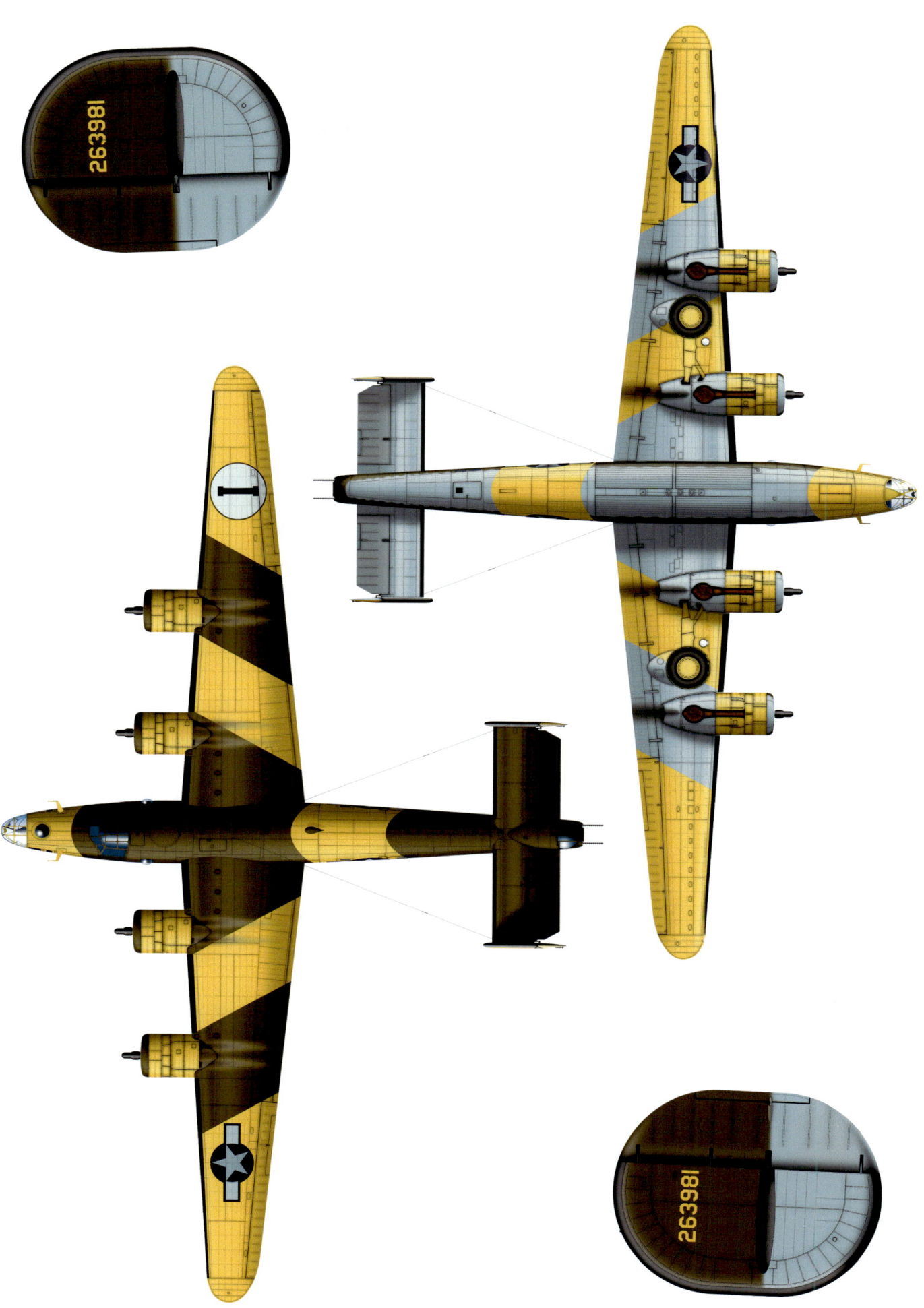

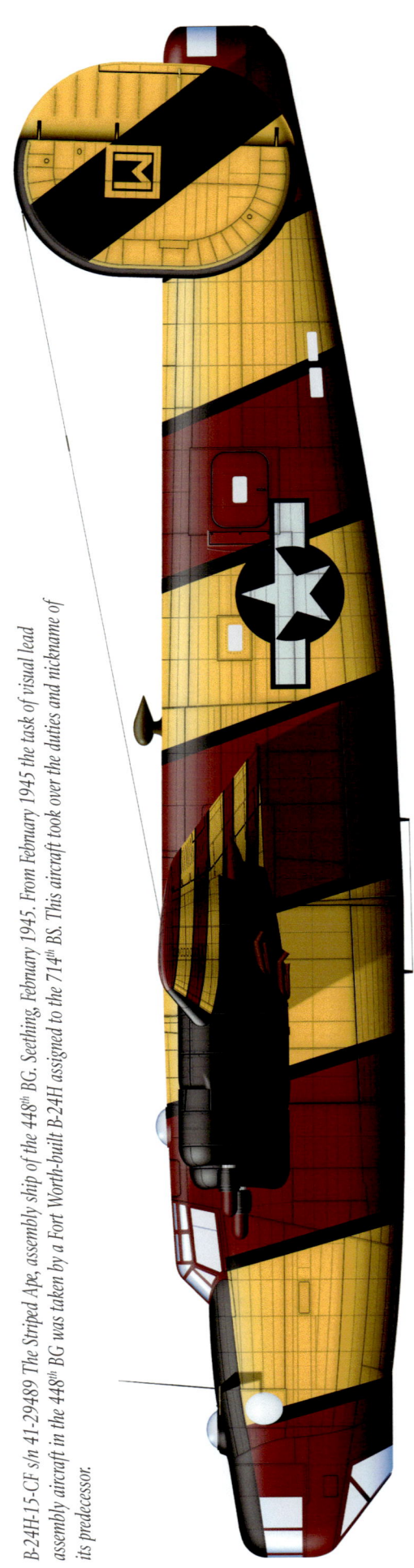

B-24H-15-CF s/n 41-29489 *The Striped Ape*, assembly ship of the 448th BG. Seething, February 1945. From February 1945 the task of visual lead assembly aircraft in the 448th BG was taken by a Fort Worth-built B-24H assigned to the 714th BS. This aircraft took over the duties and nickname of its predecessor.

The machine was lightened by deleting all the turrets, and painted diagonal semi-gloss maroon and yellow bands divided by black stripes. Engine cowlings and nacelles as well as the anti-glare panel were painted flat black. The outer surfaces of the vertical tails were painted in deep yellow with a black diagonal stripe, with the aircraft's call-letter W within the squadron square symbol superimposed on this band. It was common practice in the 448th BG to repeat the aircraft call-letter on the inner surfaces of the vertical fins. Absence of W on the inner surface of the port fin is curious, but most amazing, clearly visible is V on the inner surface of starboard fin? *The Striped Ape* was salvaged in May 1945.

136

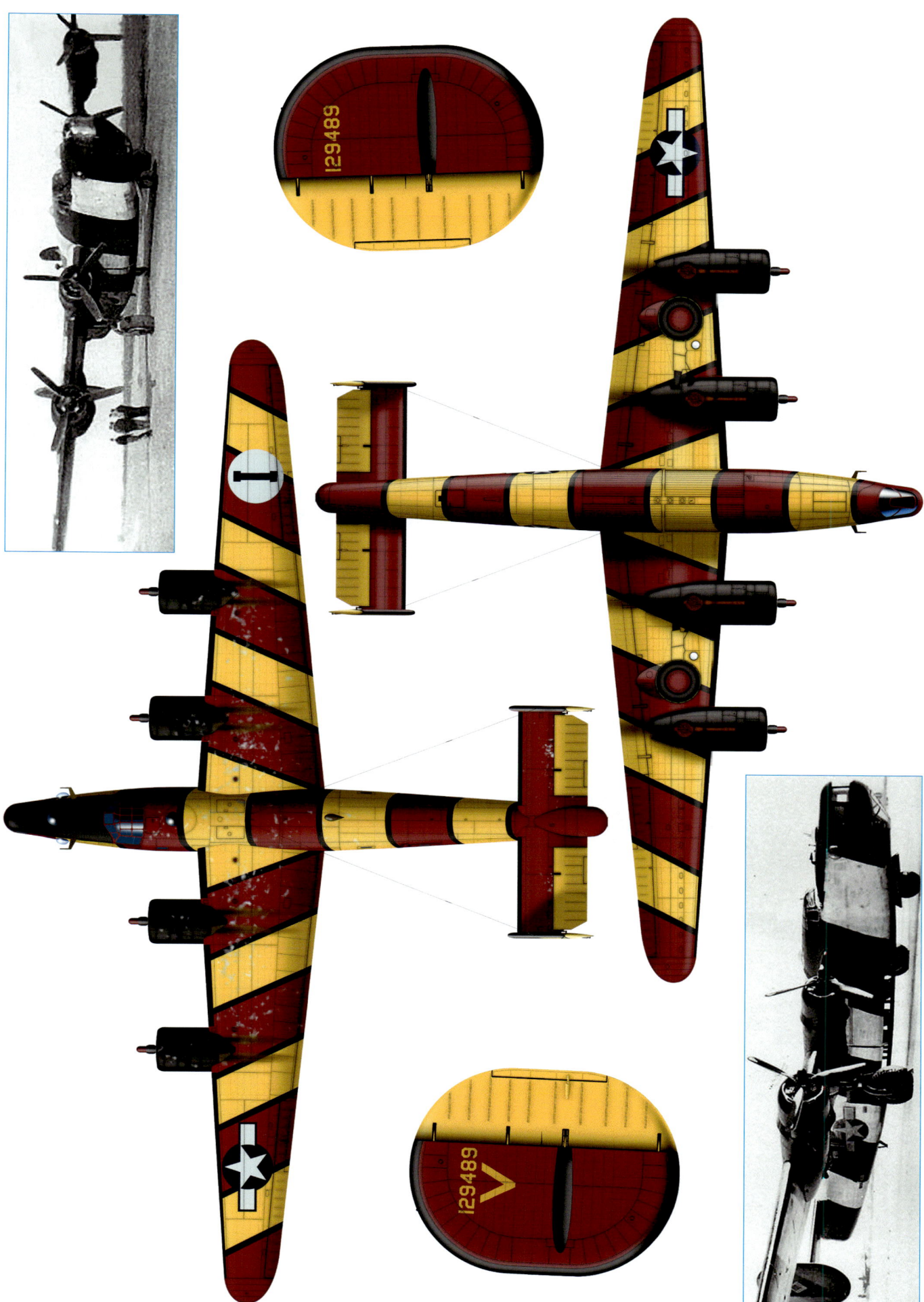

138

P-47C-5-RE s/n 41-6380, formation monitor of the 448th BG at Seething. Sometime in the summer of 1944 the 448th BG received a Thunderbolt for formation monitoring duties. As shown in the upper photo, the aircraft kept part of the invasion stripes on the lower rear fuselage. However, the condition of the Olive Drab / Neutral Grey camouflage was poor. The Olive Drab started to peel off and flaked off in many places, especially around movable components, but it also chipped off from inspection panels and the engine cowlings.

In late 1944 the aircraft was renovated. The eyes and a shark's mouth were retouched, the invasion stripes were overpainted, and the vertical tail was painted in deep yellow with a black diagonal band – the marking of the 448th BG.

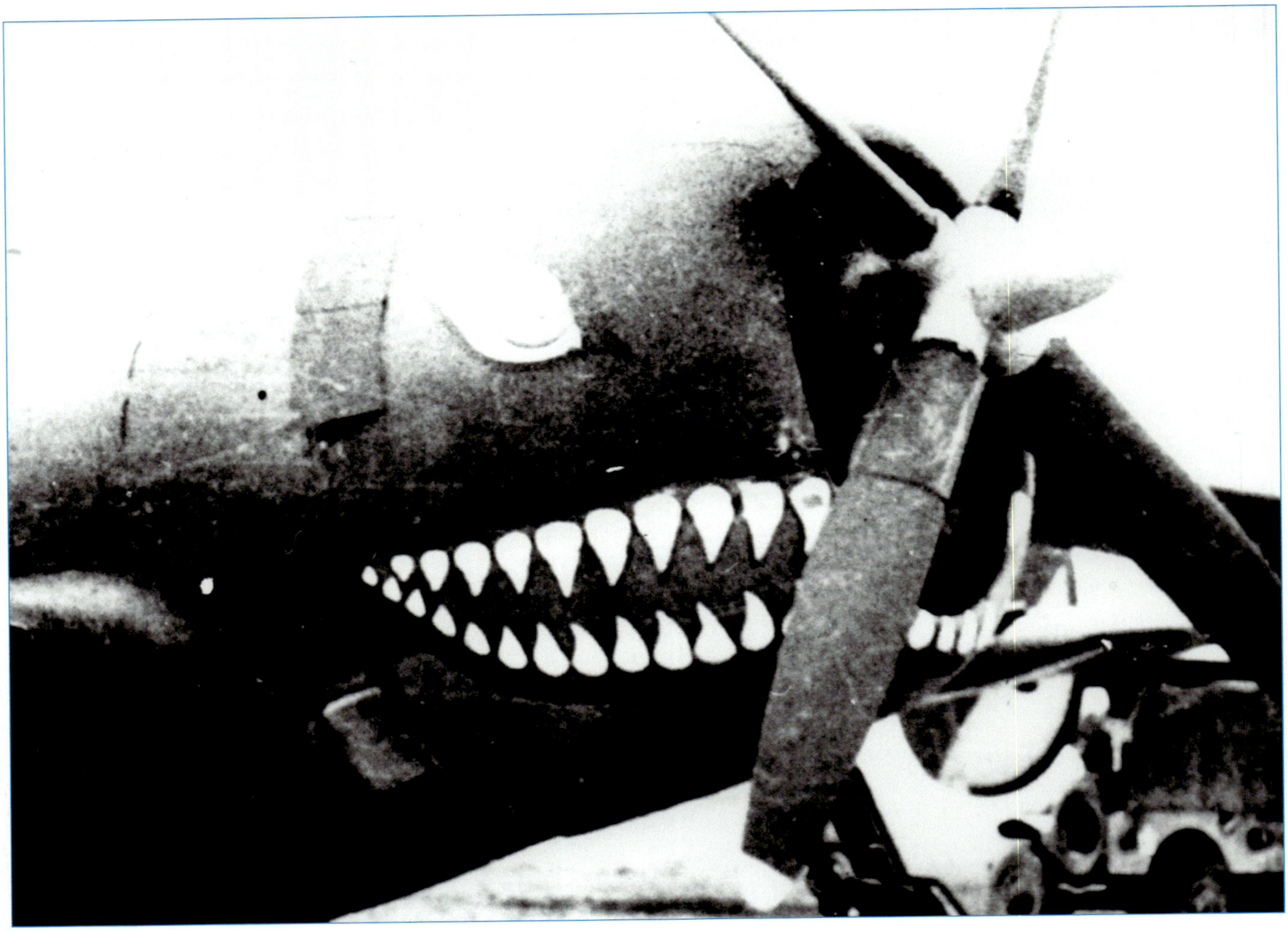

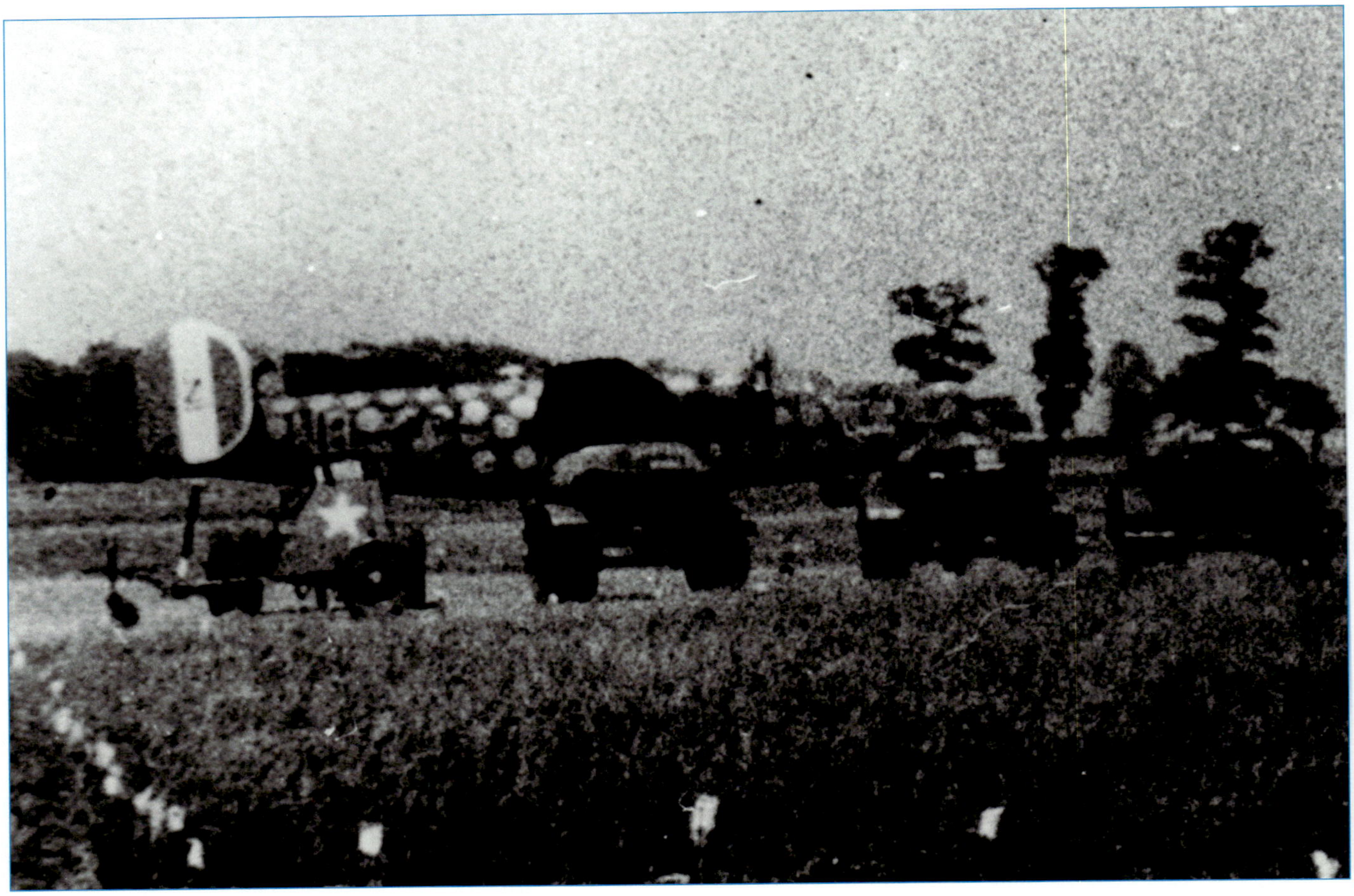

141

B-24H-1-FO s/n 42-7552 Lil' Cookie, assembly ship of the 489th BG, Halesworth, August 1944. Originally assigned to the 576th BS / 392nd BG as B the aircraft was transferred before any combat mission to the 66th BS / 44th BG and coded as K, before later being sent to the 67th BS as NB●A. Sometime in mid-1944 the war-weary Lil' Cookie was obtained by the 489th BG to become the group's 'Zebra forming plane'. It was lightened by dismantling its upper and rear turrets and on both sides of the fuselage navigational lights were fixed to create the letter 'W' along with a modified rear section carrying the cruciform signal lamp array. Initially, Lil' Cookie retained its original camouflage, except for the front de-armed turret and end fuselage sections that were painted Honey Yellow, as were the engine cowlings. The original nose art and the squadron code letters of the previous user NB were left unchanged. The outer vertical tails surfaces were painted green with a white vertical stripe (the markings of the 489th BG) with a black Z within. After the aircraft's first flight as a 'rendezvous ship' it turned out that it needed to distinguish itself further. Consequently, all surfaces were painted in yellow polka dots. The Lil' Cookie badge was repainted slightly forward in red.

Above: An unidentified airman from Lil' Cookie's crew from the time, when she served as NB●A with 67th BS.

144

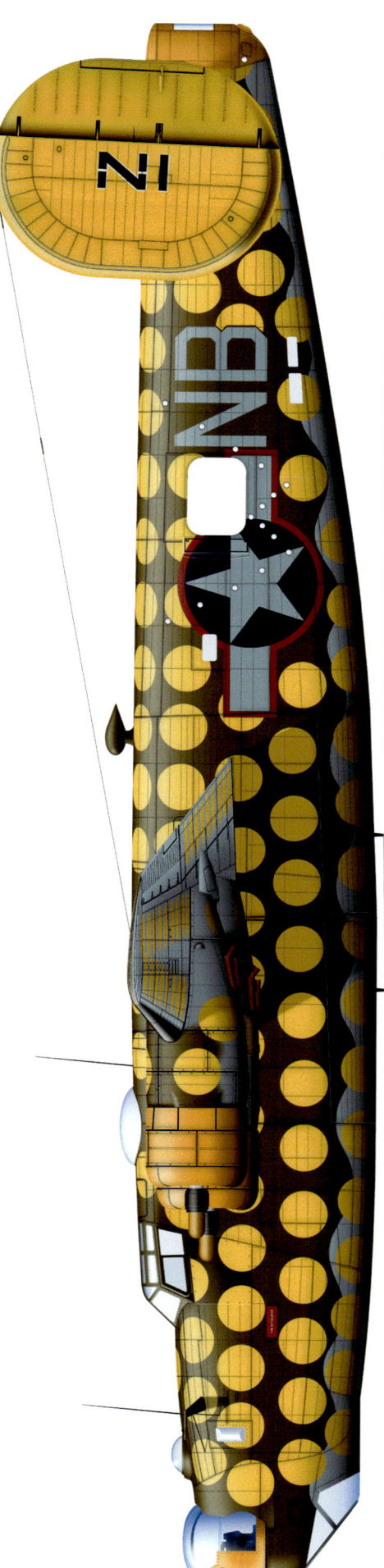

Shortly before the 489th BG returned to the USA in November 1944 to train on the new B-29 Superfortress, in late August or early September 1944, the 489th BG (originally part of the 95th CBW) was reassigned to the 20th CBW. Consequently, the vertical tails of all machines in the group, including Lil' Cookie, were repainted in deep yellow. Besides the colour of the vertical tails, no other changes in markings of this assembly ship was noticed.

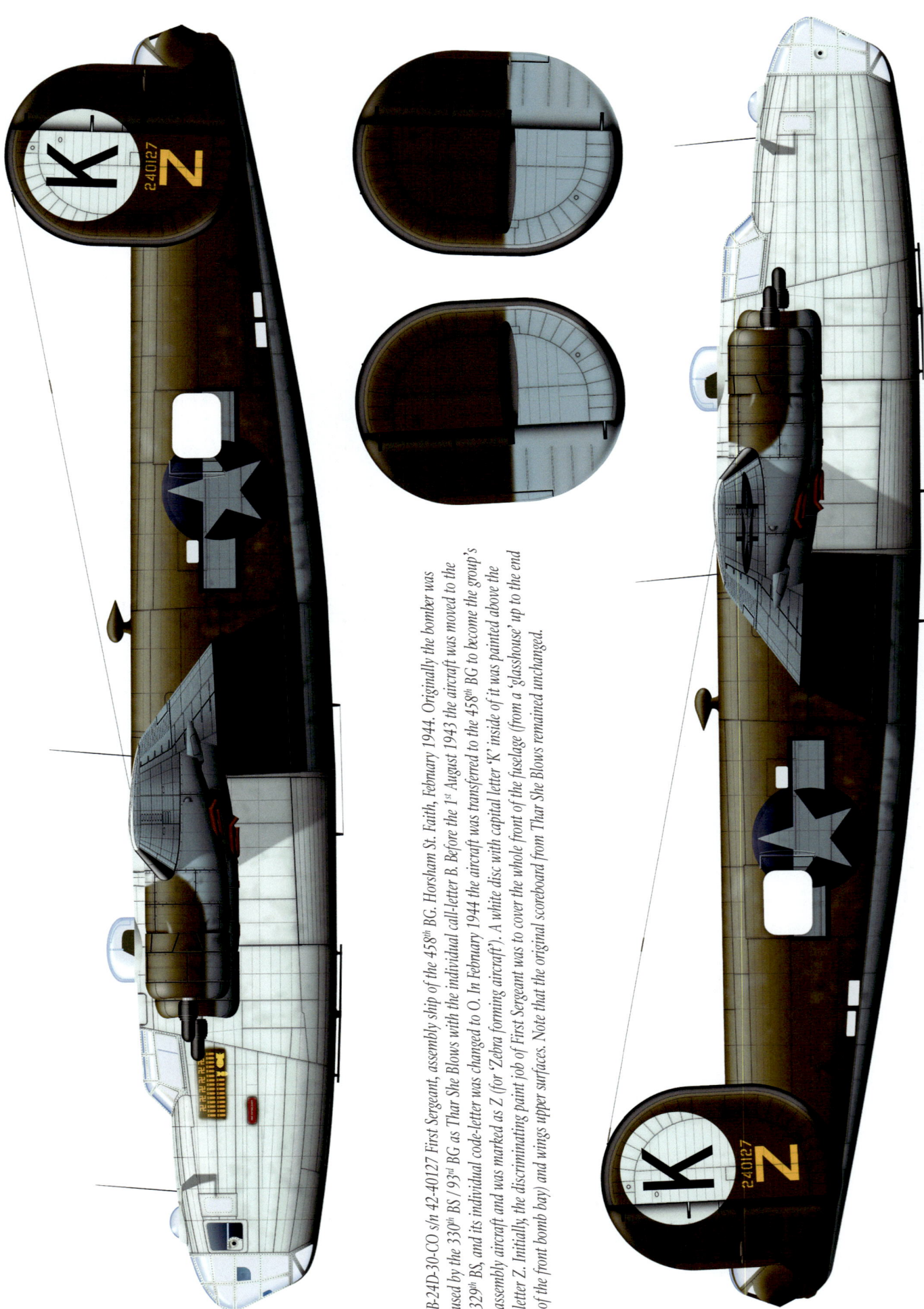

B-24D-30-CO s/n 42-40127 First Sergeant, assembly ship of the 458th BG. Horsham St. Faith, February 1944. Originally the bomber was used by the 330th BS / 93rd BG as Thar She Blows with the individual call-letter B. Before the 1st August 1943 the aircraft was moved to the 329th BS, and its individual code-letter was changed to O. In February 1944 the aircraft was transferred to the 458th BG to become the group's assembly aircraft and was marked as Z (for 'Zebra forming aircraft'). A white disc with capital letter 'K' inside of it was painted above the letter Z. Initially, the discriminating paint job of First Sergeant was to cover the whole front of the fuselage (from a 'glasshouse' up to the end of the front bomb bay) and wings upper surfaces. Note that the original scoreboard from Thar She Blows remained unchanged.

147

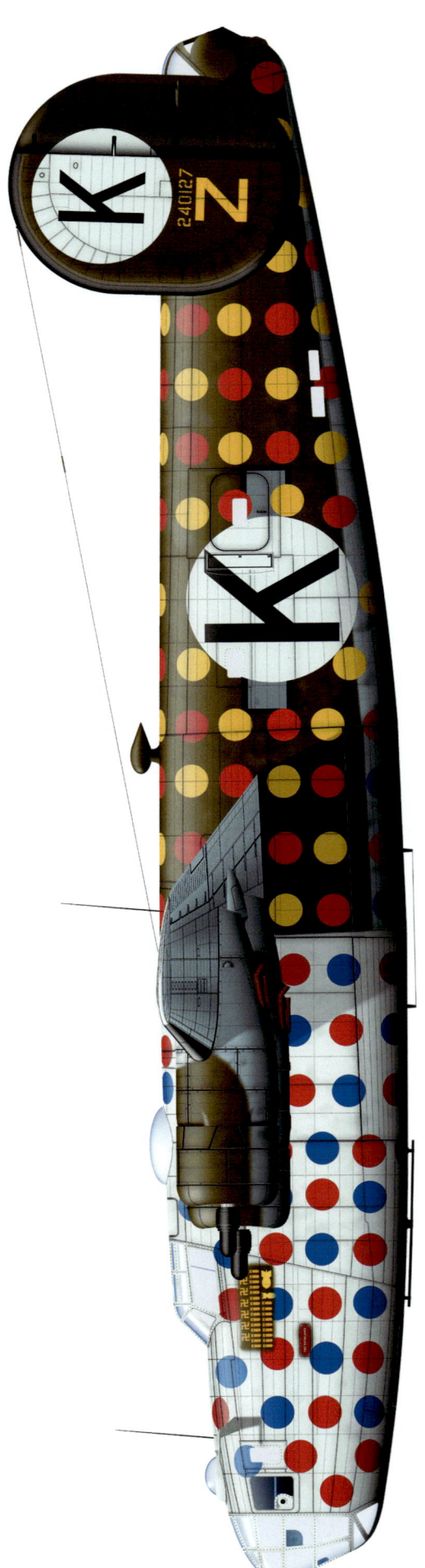

In late March 1944 First Sergeant was covered with polka dots: blue and red on previously white surfaces, whilst the rear part of the fuselage, the horizontal tail upper surface and the vertical tails inner surfaces were painted in yellow and red polka dots. Additional white discs with the letter 'K' (458th BG markings) were applied over the national insignia painted on the fuselage. Note that the top turret was replaced with an observation cupola. First Sergeant was burned out in flar accident on 27th May 1944 at Horsham St. Faith.

Above and below: A victim of a flare mishap on 27th May 1944.

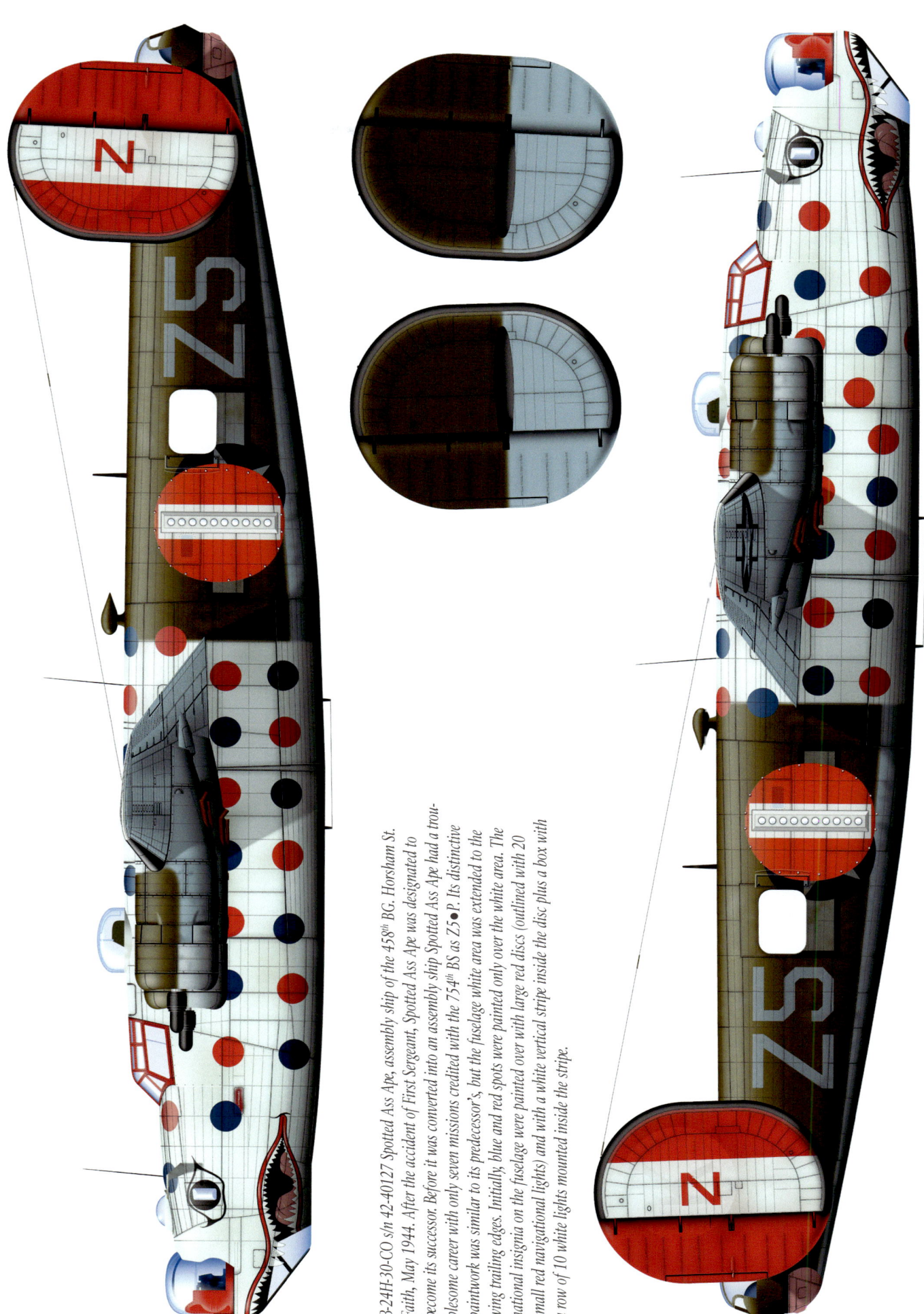

B-24H-30-CO s/n 42-40127 *Spotted Ass Ape*, assembly ship of the 458th BG. Horsham St. Faith, May 1944. After the accident of First Sergeant, *Spotted Ass Ape* was designated to become its successor. Before it was converted into an assembly ship *Spotted Ass Ape* had a troublesome career with only seven missions credited with the 754th BS as Z5●P. Its distinctive paintwork was similar to its predecessor's, but the fuselage white area was extended to the wing trailing edges. Initially, blue and red spots were painted only over the white area. The national insignia on the fuselage were painted over with large red discs (outlined with 20 small red navigational lights) and with a white vertical stripe inside the disc plus a box with a row of 10 white lights mounted inside the stripe.

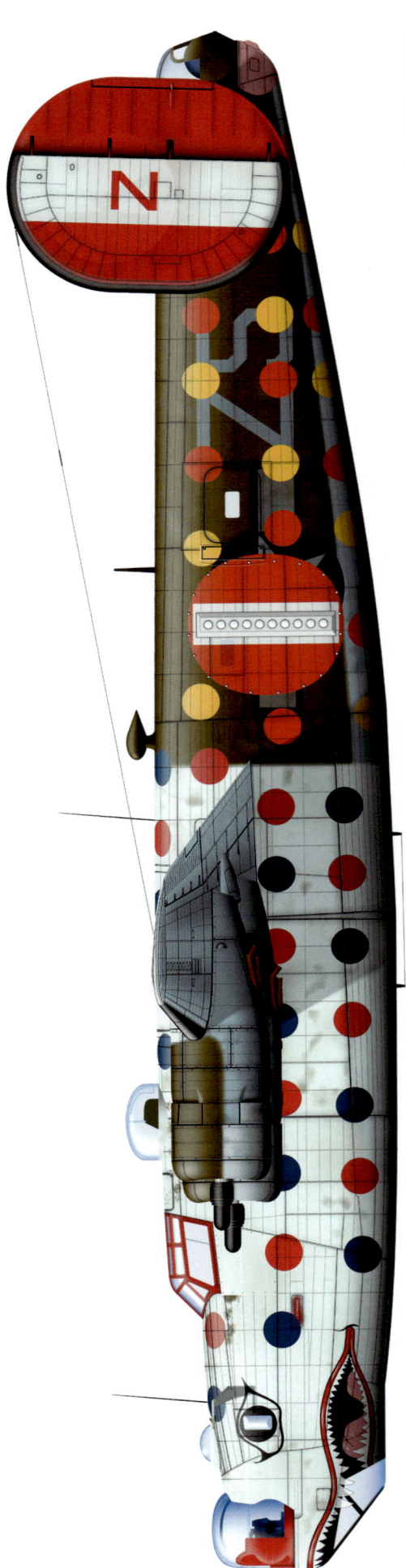

In early June 1944 red and yellow polka dots were applied over the rear fuselage sides, the horizontal tail upper surface and the vertical tails inner surfaces of Spotted Ass Ape. It is worth noting that the dots on this aircraft were painted more sparsely than those on First Sergeant. Also of note, but insignificant at first glance, are a few details, for example a lighter shade on the engine cowlings Neutral Grey, 'Skin Pink' painted below the rear turret, a white star painted on the nosewheel hub disc, and a white disc with a 'K' inside the disc showing through the red paint on the outer vertical tails surfaces. The aircraft was lost during landing on 9th March 1945 when an undercarriage leg collapsed and it crashed.

154

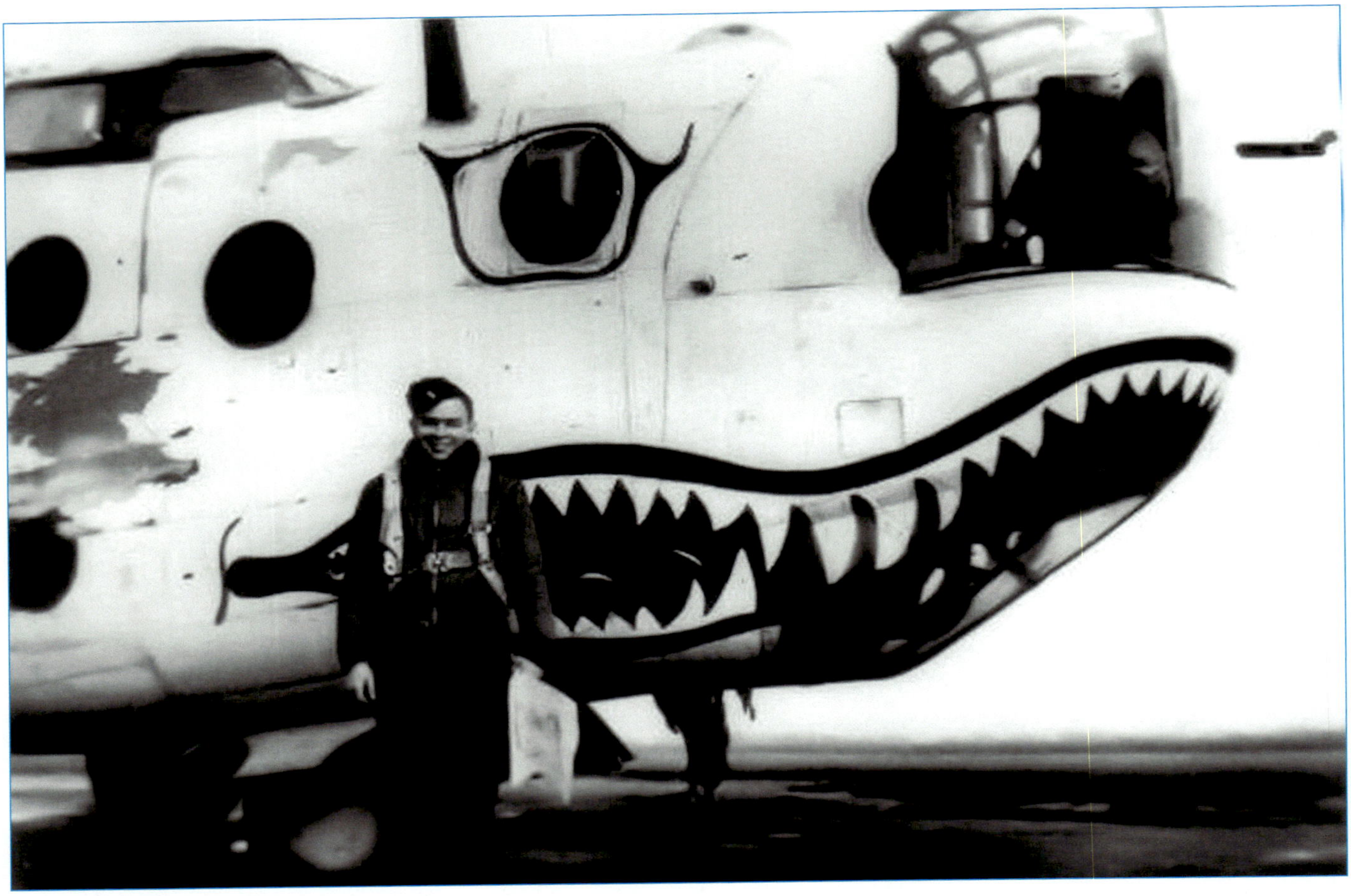

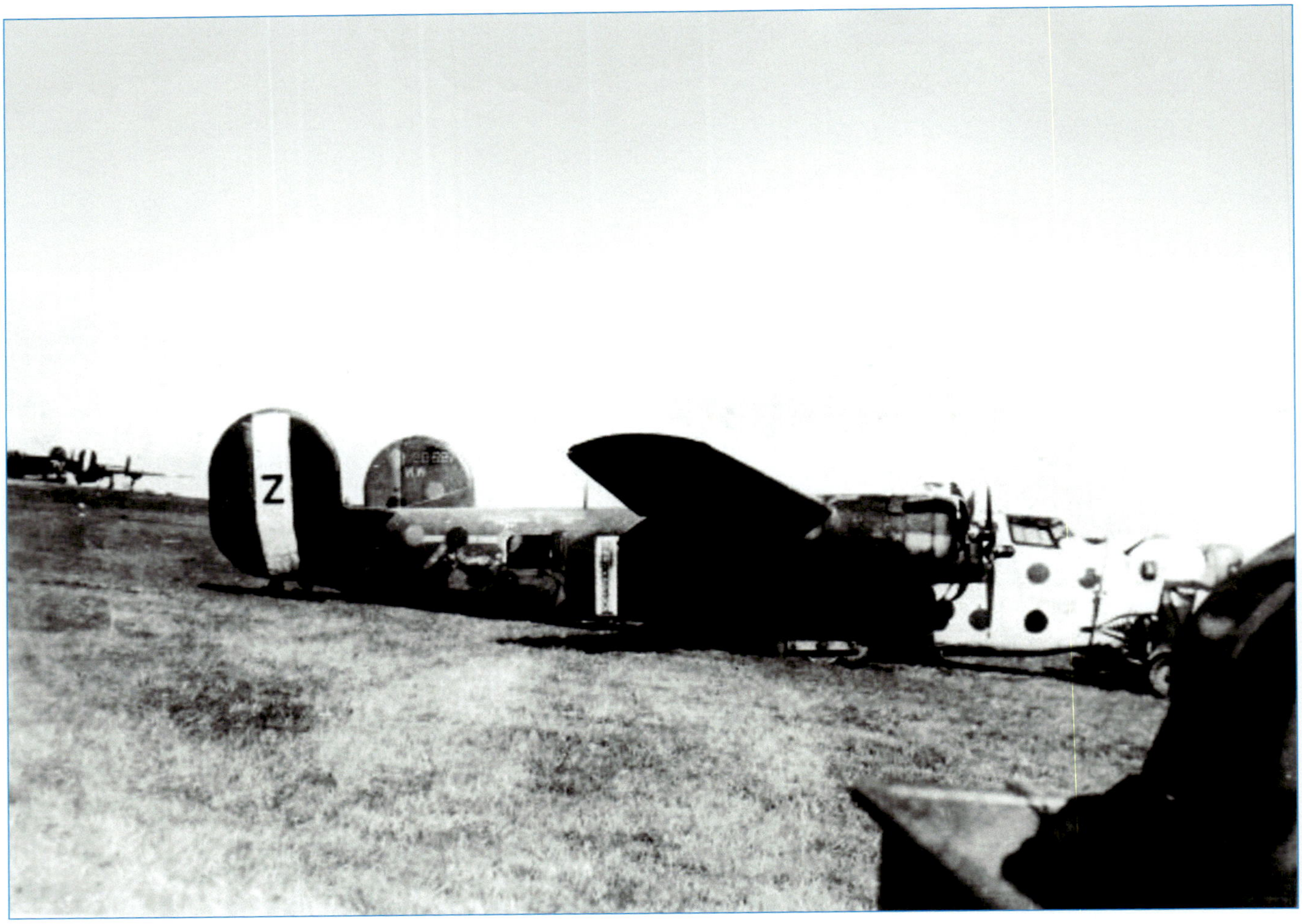
Z

157

mizpah

"CAP'N"

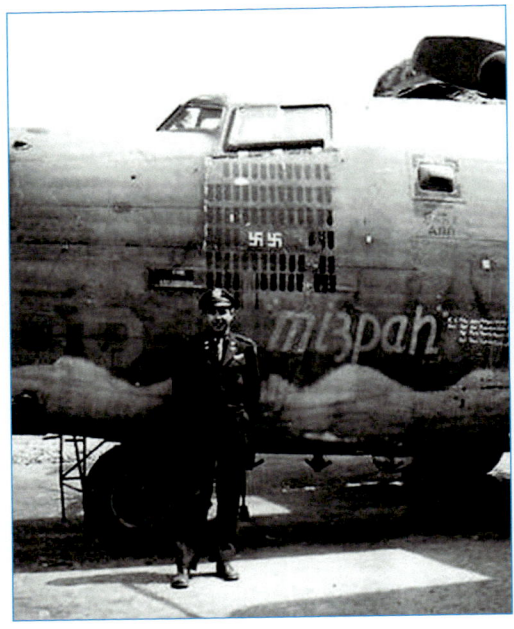

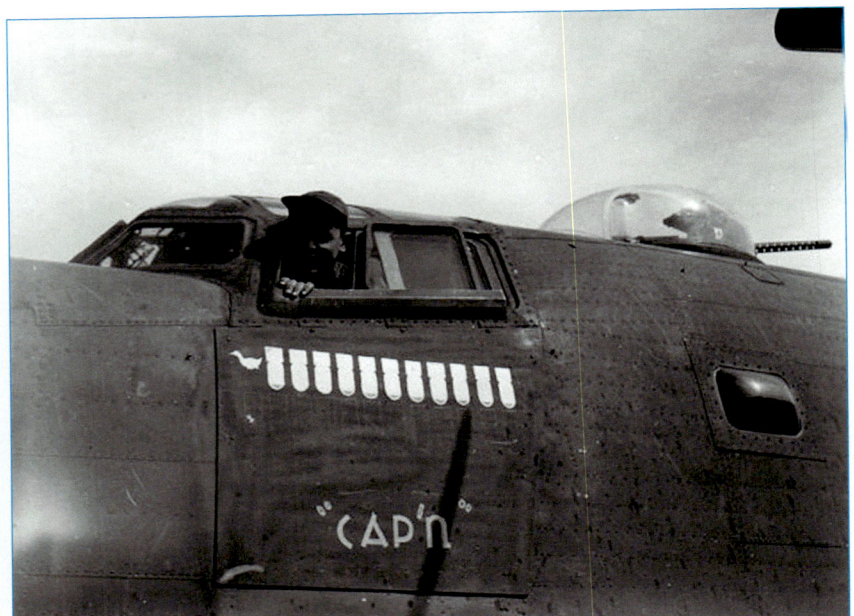

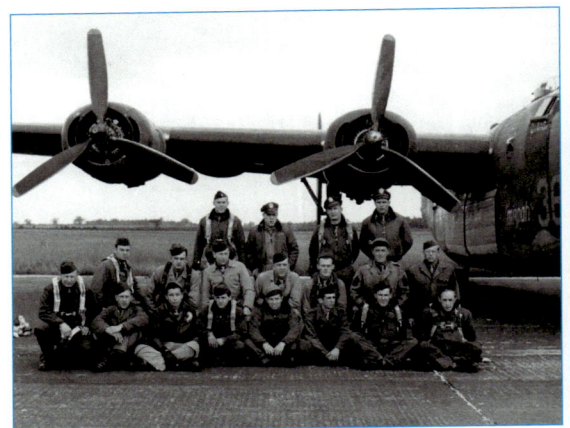

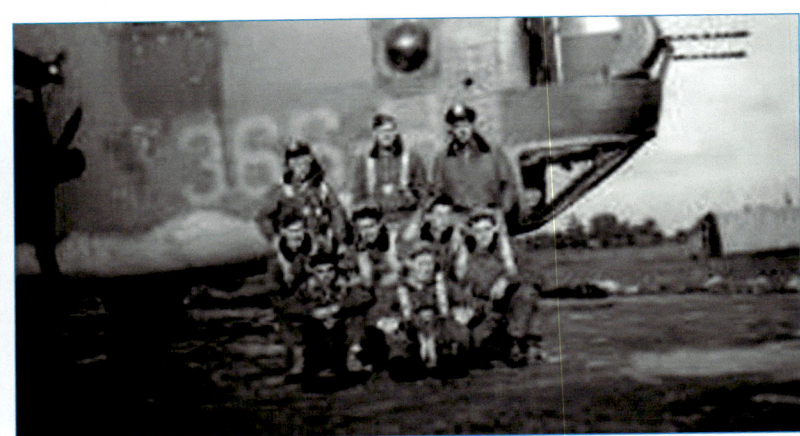

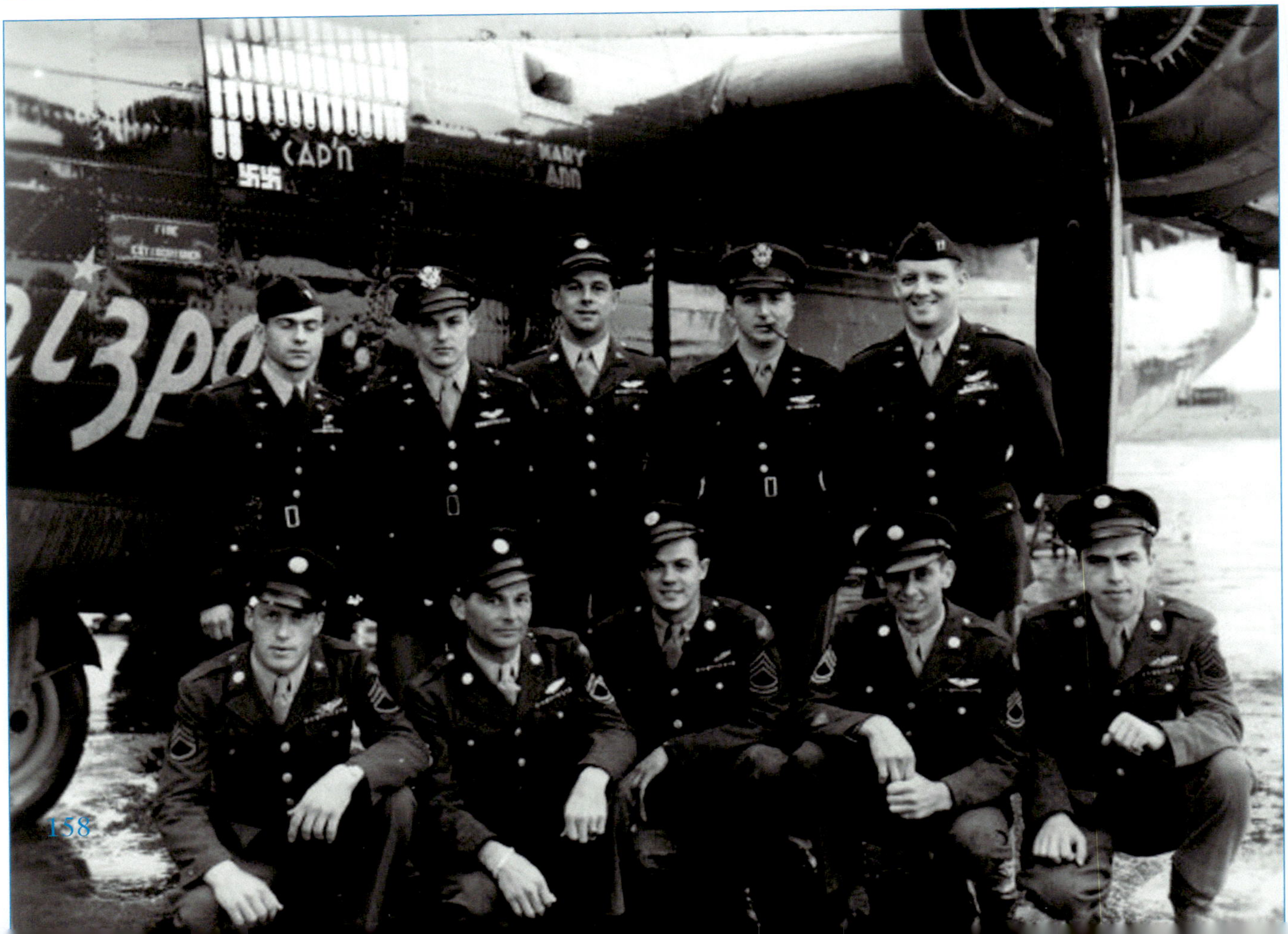
CAP'N
MARY ANN

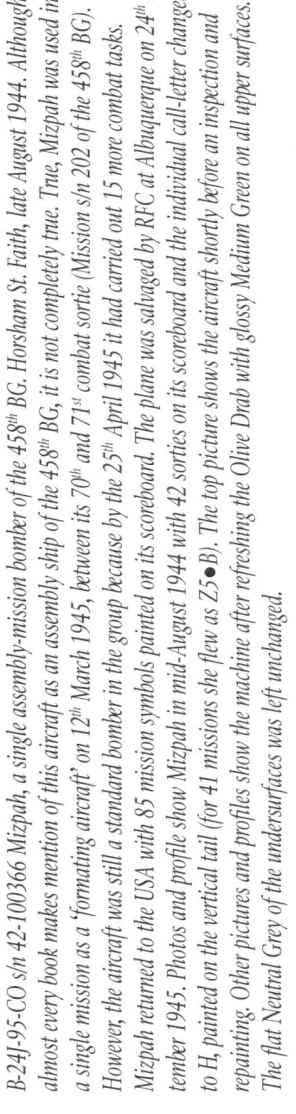

B-24J-95-CO s/n 42-100366 Mizpah, a single assembly-mission bomber of the 458th BG. Horsham St. Faith, late August 1944. Although almost every book makes mention of this aircraft as an assembly ship of the 458th BG, it is not completely true. True, Mizpah was used in a single mission as a 'formating aircraft' on 12th March 1945, between its 70th and 71st combat sortie (Mission s/n 202 of the 458th BG). However, the aircraft was still a standard bomber in the group because by the 25th April 1945 it had carried out 15 more combat tasks. Mizpah returned to the USA with 85 mission symbols painted on its scoreboard. The plane was salvaged by RFC at Albuquerque on 24th September 1945. Photos and profile show Mizpah in mid-August 1944 with 42 sorties on its scoreboard and the individual call-letter changed to H, painted on the vertical tail (for 41 missions she flew as Z5●B). The top picture shows the aircraft shortly before an inspection and repainting. Other pictures and profiles show the machine after refreshing the Olive Drab with glossy Medium Green on all upper surfaces. The flat Neutral Grey of the undersurfaces was left unchanged.

On 27th May 27 1944, the group was assembling over Cromer for a mission to Neunkirchen, and had just completed a left turn and were making a right turn when the pilot of B-24H 42-95159 Rough Riders II, 2Lt Howard Lobo, either did not or could not complete the turn rapidly enough and collided with another Liberator 42-95183 Briney Marlin piloted by 2Lt Lester Martin. The impact tore the entire tail assembly from s/n 159 and that aircraft was last seen spinning down into the under cast about five miles offshore into the North Sea. All ten men aboard were listed as MIA and later declared dead. Two bodies were recovered after washing ashore – those of the navigator and bombardier. Aboard Briney Marlin (s/n 183) that day, as a fill in top turret gunner/flight engineer, was S/Sgt Chester R. Carlstrum, the tail gunner on Crew 74 (he was also qualified as a flight engineer). When the collision occurred, 2Lt Martin rang the bail out bell. Carlstrum dropped down and opened the bomb bay and salvoed the bomb load. He then bailed out through the bomb bay. The tail gunner S/Sgt Wilbert Abshire, also a fill in crewman that day from Crew 75, bailed out from the tail section. In the few seconds between collision and the two men bailing out, the ship had lost several thousand feet of altitude. 2Lt Martin was able to regain control and he rescinded his bail out order. The impact had bent about 6-8 feet of the right wing of Briney Marlin down at a 90° angle (see photos). They radioed the control tower at Horsham and asked for instructions. Colonel Isbell took off in Ginny, the group's P-47, tolook over the B-24 from the air. He ordered Martin to point the aircraft out to sea and bail the crew out. Martin decided he had enough control and decided instead, to attempt a landing at base. Keeping the airspeed high, they were able to land without further incident. As they were over the North Sea when the accident happened, Carlstrum and Abshire were never found, and presumably drowned in the English Channel. They are both listed at Cambridge on the Tablets of the Missing. Lester Martin gives a lot of credit to Carlstrum for saving the plane that day. His quick action in releasing the bomb load is believed to have been one of the factors that helped Martin regain control of the aircraft.

P-47D-25-RE s/n 42-26560 *Ginny*, formation monitor of the 458th BG, Horsham St. Faith, spring of 1945. The photo above shows Col. James Isbell, CO of the 458th BG, taxiing *Ginny* before flight.

B-24D s/n 41-24109, assembly aircraft of the 466th BG. The photo above was taken sometime in March, and the picture below in April 1944

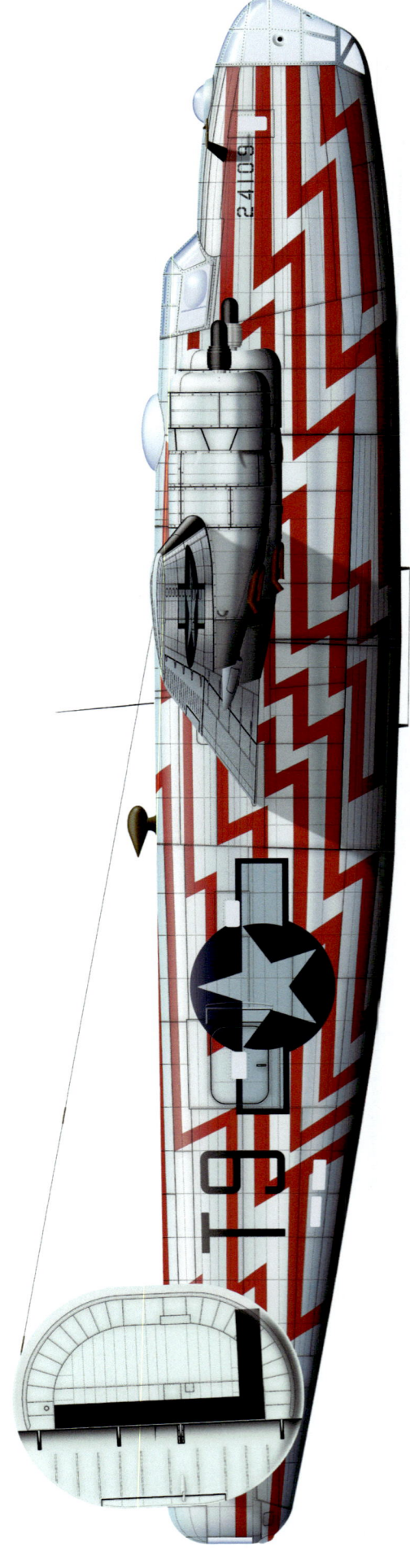

B-24D-20-CO s/n 41-24109 '109', assembly ship of the 466th BG, Attlebridge, May 1944. Originally as Ready & Willing it was an aircraft of the 330th BS / 93rd BG. Marked as C the aircraft took part in operation 'Tidal Wave' (attack on the Ploesti Oil Refinery complex) on 1st August 1943, where it was the last machine to fly over the target. After returning to the UK it was still in the 93rd BG based at Hardwick and performed 37 combat sorties with 'Ted's Travelling Circus'. In March 1944 the war-weary bomber was transferred to the 466th BG, and was designated to become a formation assembly aircraft. The aircraft was lightened by dismantling the turrets (the upper turret was replaced with an observation cupola, and the rear section was faired over) and stripped of paint from all surfaces. Initially, it was not even painted, except a black code T9 situated on the rear fuselage, and large letters 'L' on the outer parts of the vertical tails. There was also a serial number painted on the nose section. The 'new' assembly aircraft of the 466th BG was ready for the job in March 1944, as it is shown in the photograph on the opposite page. However, soon after its first flight, decorative 'zigzags' or 'lightning' motifs were added on the fuselage. Additionally, the 'L' on the vertical tails was given a white background and the inner surfaces of vertical tails were also painted white. Note that the 'zigzags' ARE NOT symmetrical!

163

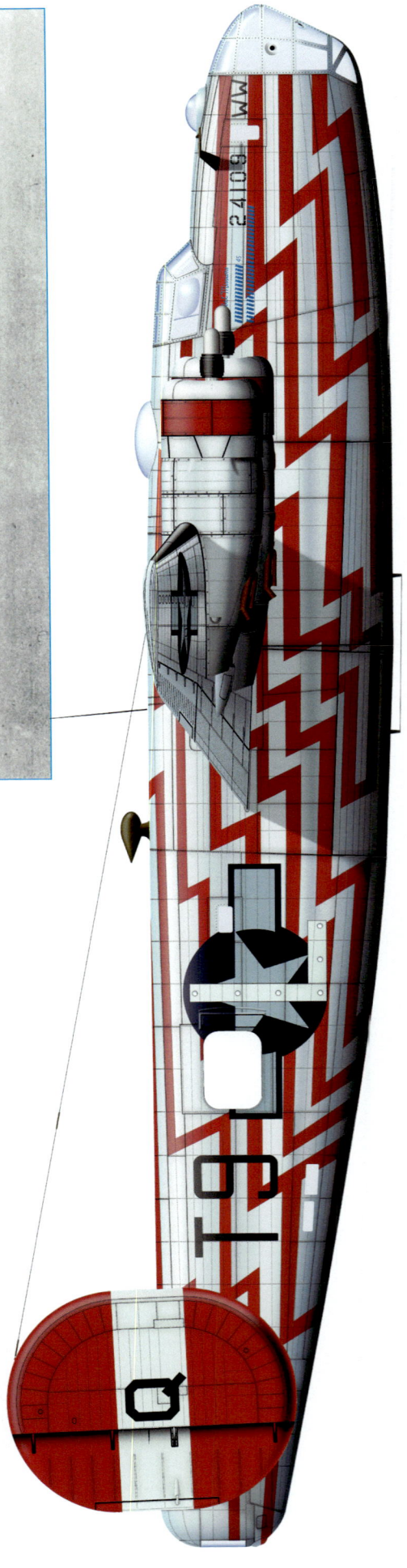

In May 1944 the outer vertical tail surfaces of all aircraft within the 466th BG were painted red with a white horizontal stripe. At the time few changes were made in the paintwork of '109'. An individual call-letter Q was applied on the outer vertical tails, whilst the serial numbers were painted on the inner vertical tails. A large white 'L' (the 466th BG insignia letter) was painted over the national markings on the fuselage, and signal lights were situated inside the letter. The engine cowlings were painted red, and the propeller hub spinners were painted white. On both sides, just below the cockpit, Ready & Willing successes were reproduced in a dark, probably blue, colour. On the starboard side of nose 'WW' were added after the serial number. Note that the front part of No. 2 engine's cowling was taken from another Liberator and still had its original Olive Drab / Neutral Grey camouflage. Ready & Willing also known as '109' was scrapped at Watton in May 1945.

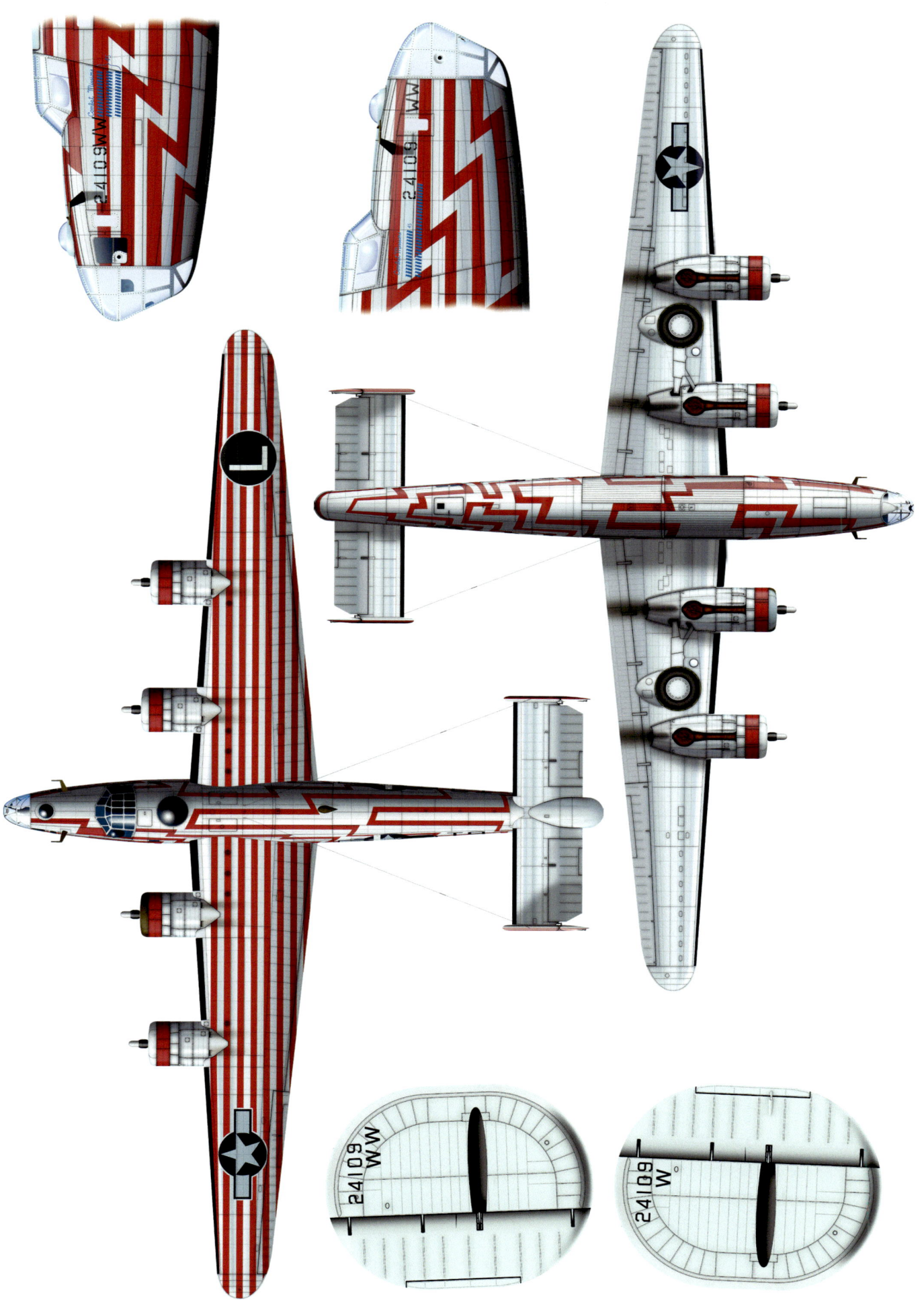

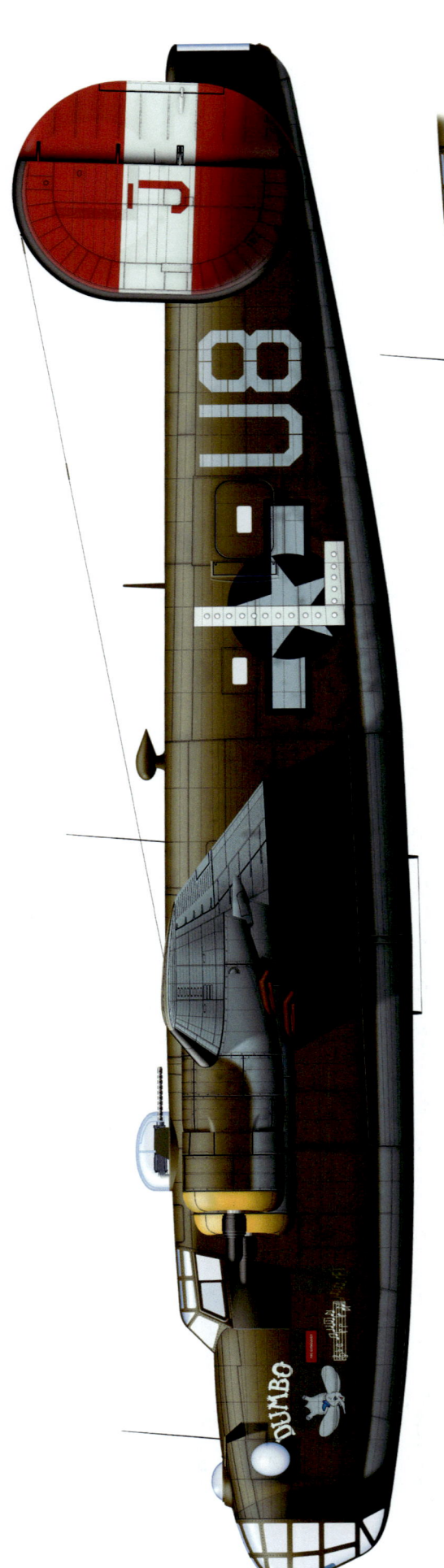
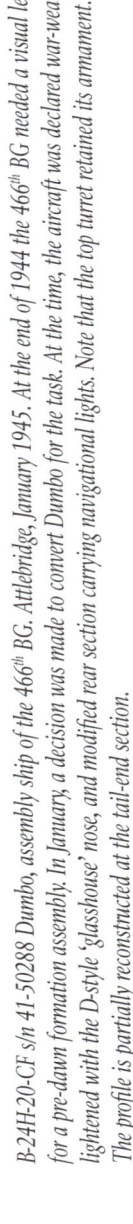

B-24H-20-CF s/n 41-50288 *Dumbo*, assembly ship of the 466th BG, Attlebridge, January 1945. At the end of 1944 the 466th BG needed a visual lead aircraft for a pre-dawn formation assembly. In January, a decision was made to convert *Dumbo* for the task. At the time, the aircraft was declared war-weary. It was lightened with the D-style 'glasshouse' nose, and modified rear section carrying navigational lights. Note that the top turret retained its armament. The profile is partially reconstructed at the tail-end section.

P-47D-11-RE, s/n 42-75517 Sally, formation monitor of the 466th BG. Attlebridge, late 1944. The plane was taken from 492nd BG, and first days with 466's flew with repainted only verical tail and keep it's original name 'LuLu'. Pilots who flown it called her 'Betsy'. During Autumn 1944 she was finally re-christianized as 'Sally' and that was the name applied on the repainted engine's cowlings.

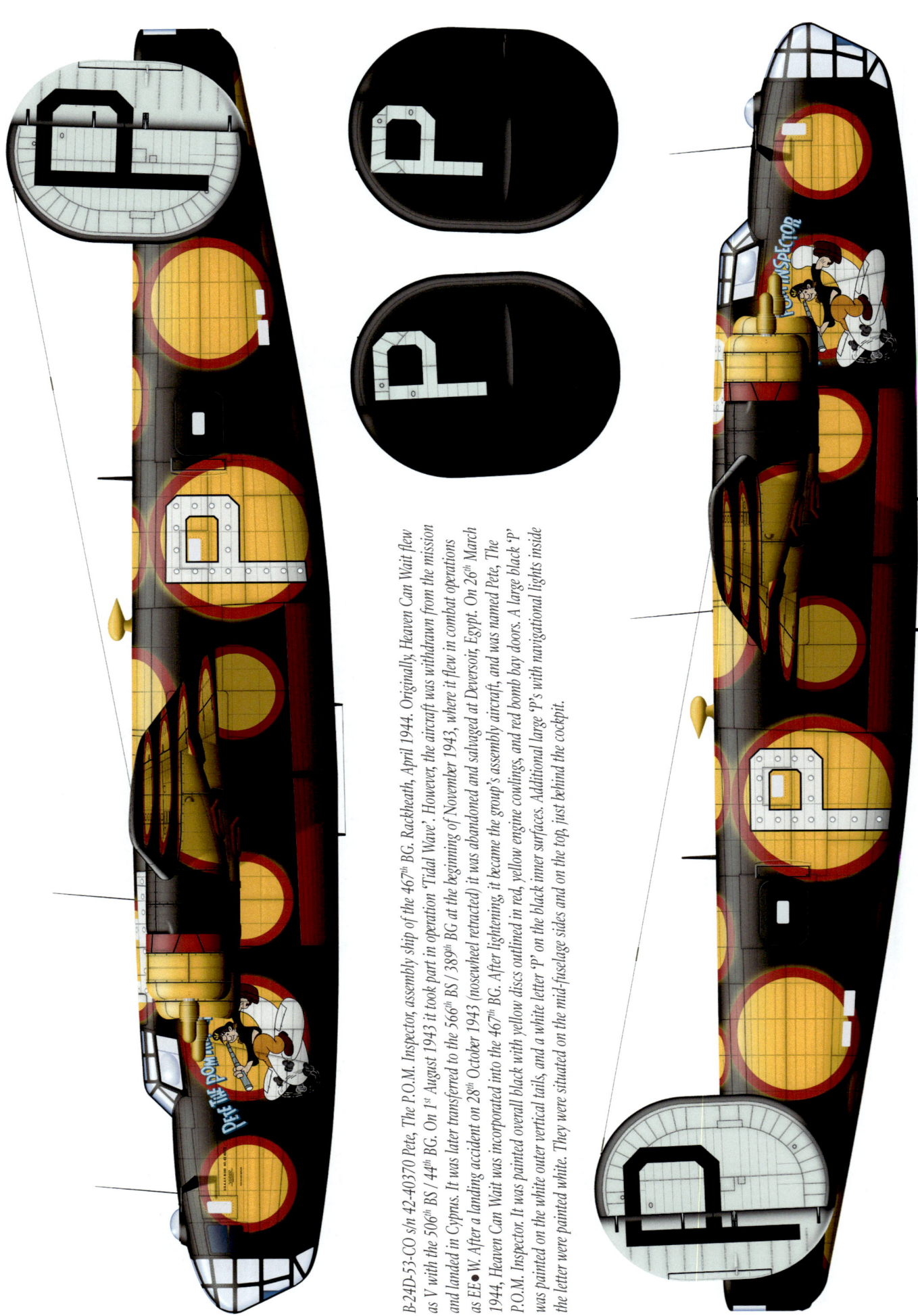

B-24D-53-CO s/n 42-40370 Pete, The P.O.M. Inspector, assembly ship of the 467th BG. Rackheath, April 1944. Originally, Heaven Can Wait flew as V with the 506th BS / 44th BG. On 1st August 1943 it took part in operation 'Tidal Wave'. However, the aircraft was withdrawn from the mission and landed in Cyprus. It was later transferred to the 566th BS / 389th BG at the beginning of November 1943, where it flew in combat operations as EE●W. After a landing accident on 28th October 1943 (nosewheel retracted) it was abandoned and salvaged at Deversoir, Egypt. On 26th March 1944, Heaven Can Wait was incorporated into the 467th BG. After lightening, it became the group's assembly aircraft, and was named Pete, The P.O.M. Inspector. It was painted overall black with yellow discs outlined in red, yellow engine cowlings, and red bomb bay doors. A large black 'P' was painted on the white outer vertical tails, and a white letter 'P' on the black inner surfaces. Additional large 'P's with navigational lights inside the letter were painted white. They were situated on the mid-fuselage sides and on the top, just behind the cockpit.

170

In May 1944, the outer vertical tails of Pete, The P.O.M. Inspector were overpainted in red with white diagonal stripes. The new layer of paint was very thin and the previous paintwork was visible through it. The 'P's applied on the inner surfaces of vertical tails were overpainted with black and replaced with the serial number in white. Note that the original Heaven Can Wait 'glasshouse' nose was converted to carry twin 0.50in Brownings. Pete, The P.O.M. Inspector, was salvaged at Rackheath in October 1944, following a landing accident with a retracted nosewheel (again!).

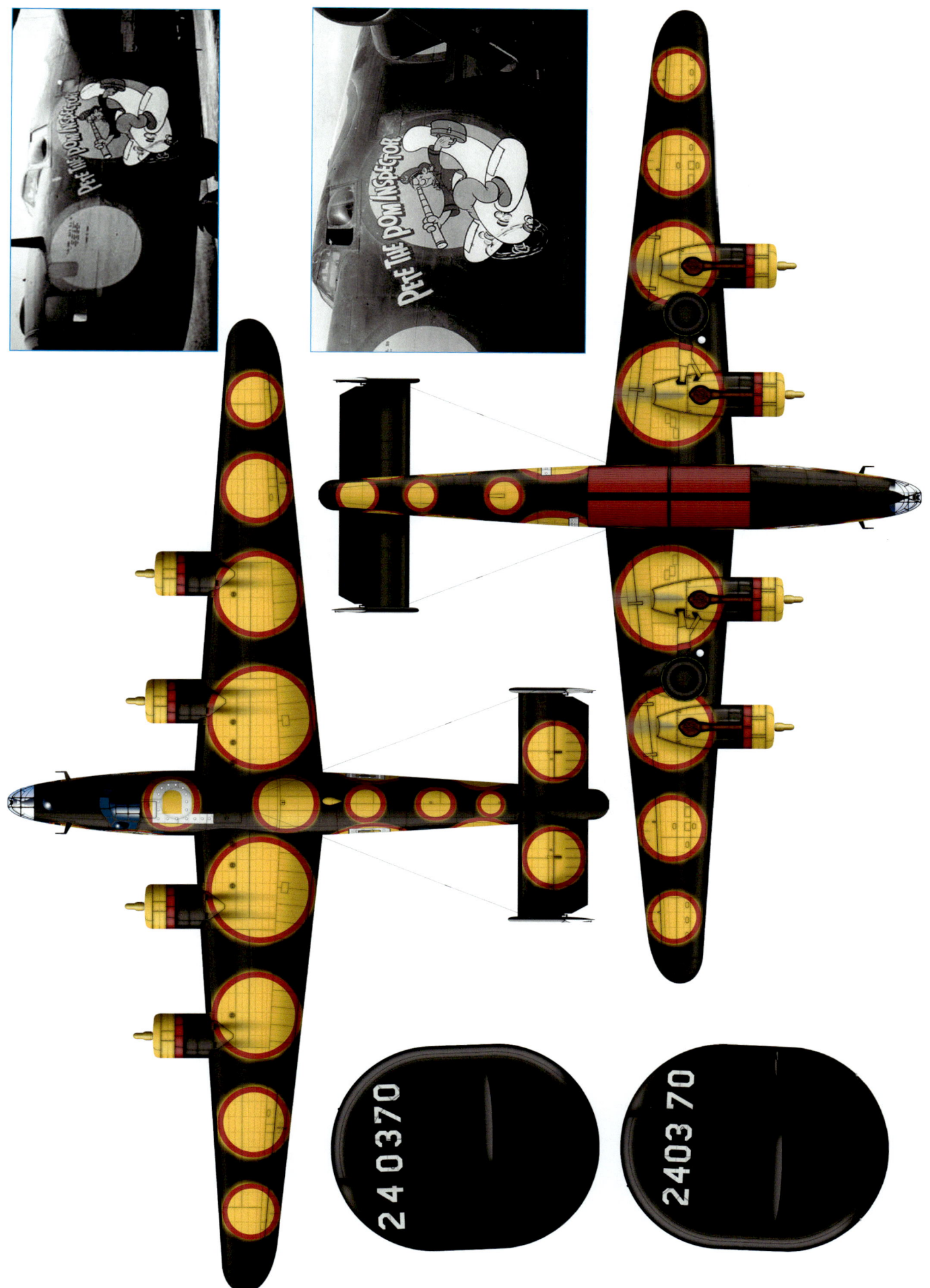

174

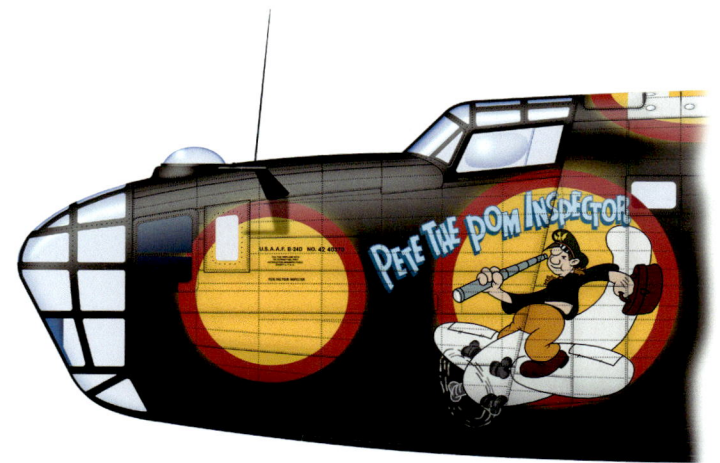

Portside paint job details and nose section differences between s/n 42-40370 Pete, The P.O.M. Inspector and s/n 41-29393 Pete, The P.O.M. Inspector 2nd.

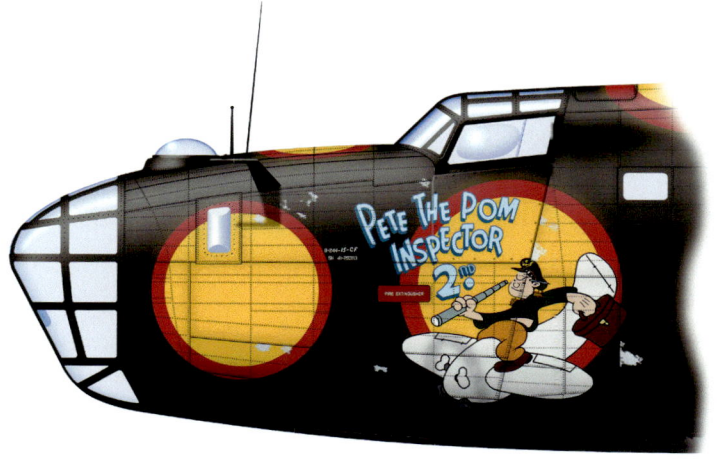

Starboard side paint job details and nose section differences between s/n 42-40370 Pete, The P.O.M. Inspector and s/n 41-29393 Pete, The P.O.M. Inspector 2nd.

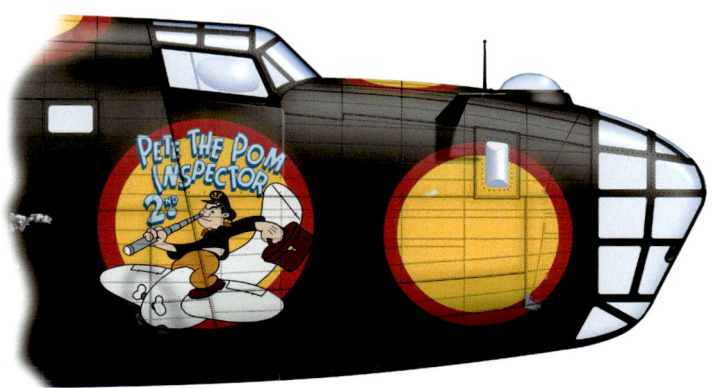

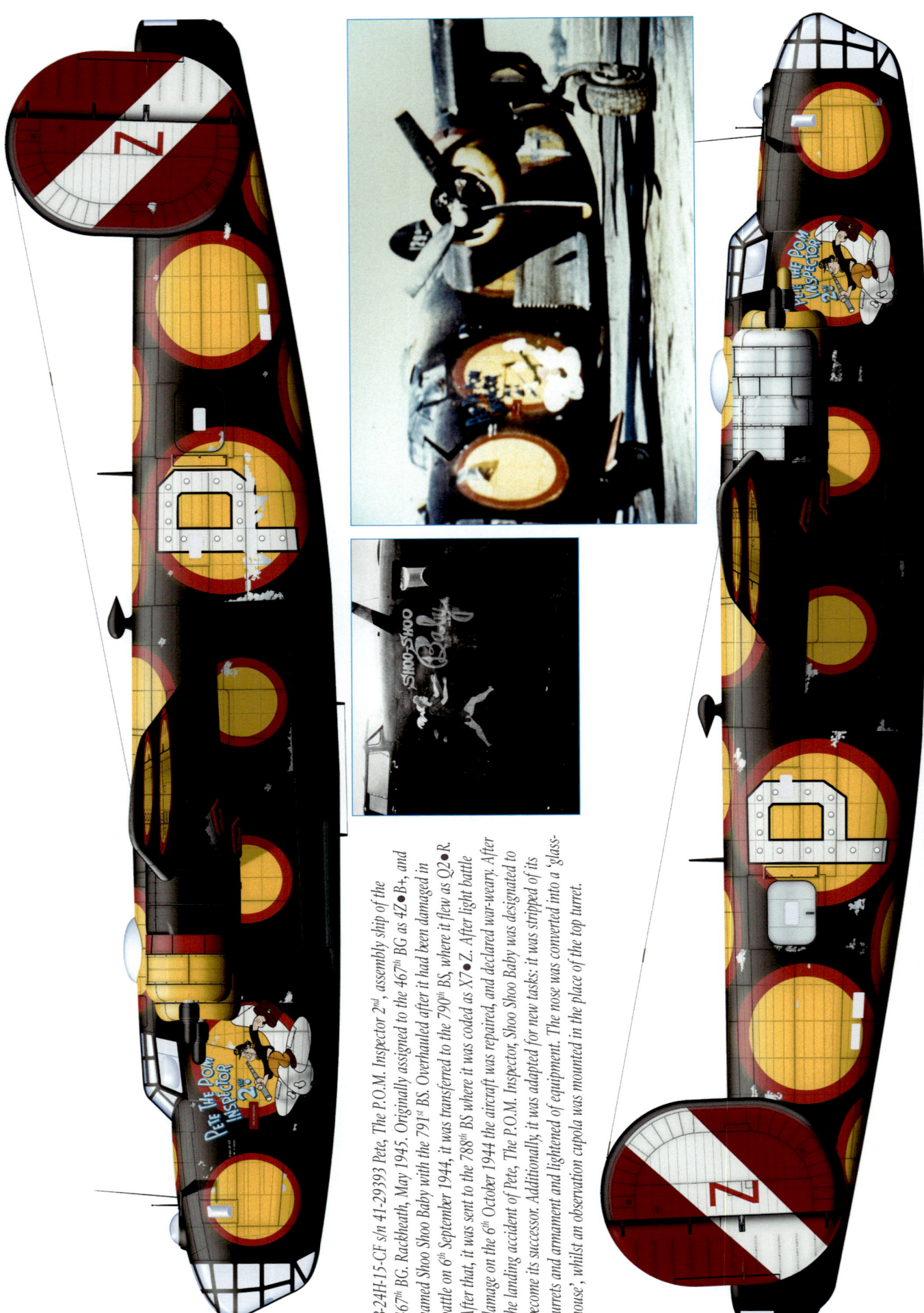

B-24H-15-CF s/n 41-29393 Pete, The P.O.M. Inspector 2nd, assembly ship of the 467th BG. Rackheath, May 1945. Originally assigned to the 467th BG as 4Z●B+, and named Shoo Shoo Baby with the 791st BS. Overhauled after it had been damaged in battle on 6th September 1944, it was transferred to the 790th BS, where it flew as Q2●R. After that, it was sent to the 788th BS where it was coded as X7●Z. After light battle damage on the 6th October 1944 the aircraft was repaired, and declared war-weary. After the landing accident of Pete, The P.O.M. Inspector, Shoo Shoo Baby was designated to become its successor. Additionally, it was adapted for new tasks: it was stripped of its turrets and armament and lightened of equipment. The nose was converted into a 'glass-house', whilst an observation cupola was mounted in the place of the top turret.

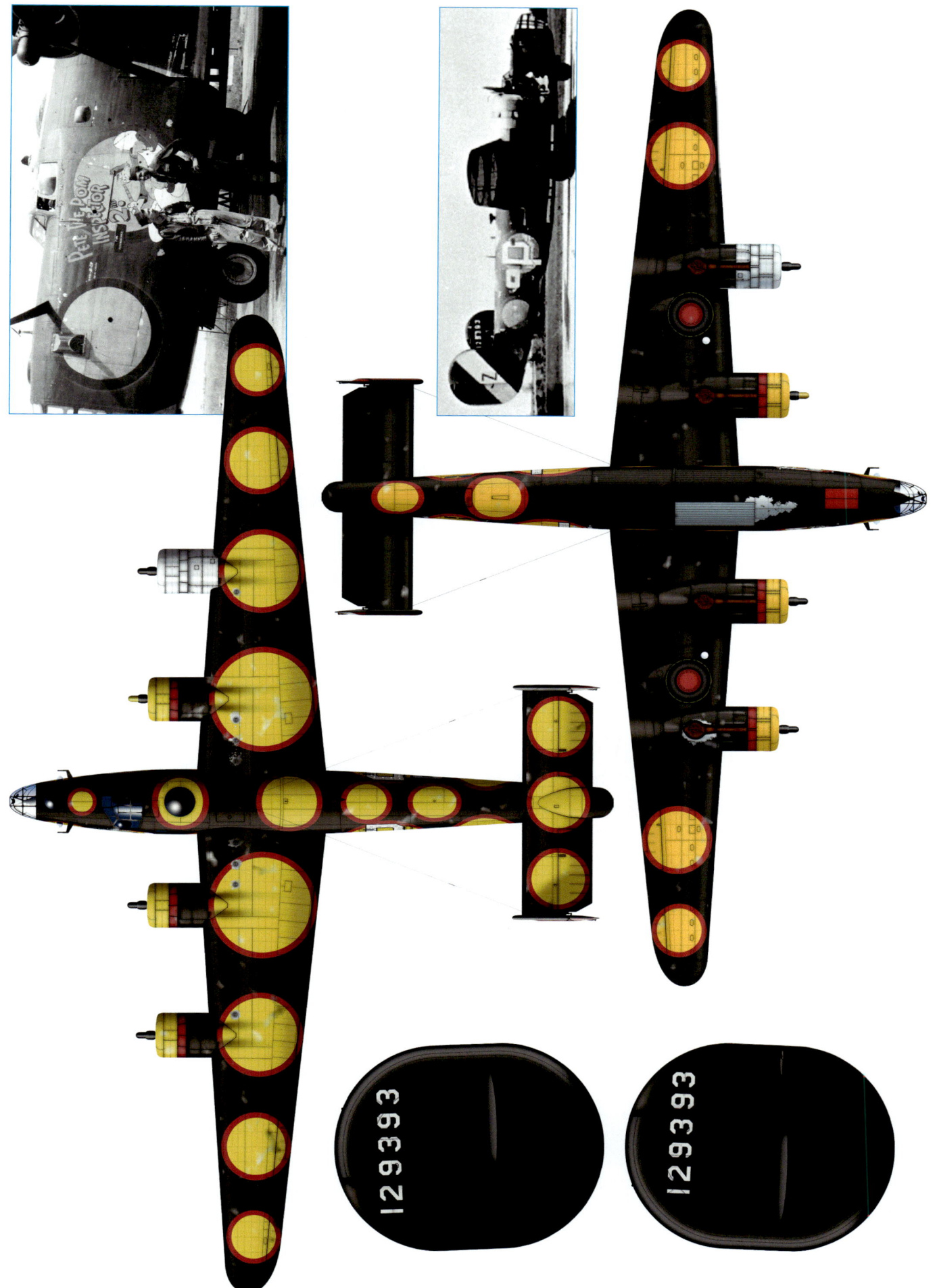

P-47D-23-RA s/n 42-27790 Little Pete, the formation monitor of the 467th BG. Rackheath, summer of 1944. Little Pete was assigned as the formation monitor to the Headquarters of the 467th BG. It was lost in a mid-air collision during a practice mission in August 1944 while flown by Lt. Col. Walter R. Smith, Group Operations Officer.

P-47D-23-RA s/n 42-27790 Little Pete, formation monitor of the 467th BG. Rackheath, summer of 1944. In the right upper corner of the picture you can see Thunderbolt at work – in close flight with B-24H s/n 42-52375 Lil' Peach of 791st BS. The aircraft was primarily flown by Col. Shower, Lt. Col. Mahoney, and formerly Lt. Col. Walter R. Smith, Group Operations Officer. The Little Pete was involved in a mid-air collision during a practice mission in August 1944 while flown by Lt. Col. Smith.

P-47D-25-RE s/n 42-26393 Little Pete 2, formation monitor of the 467th BG. Rackheath, January 1945. After Little Pete was lost, the 467th BG received another Thunderbolt designated for formation assembly monitoring duties. Named Little Pete 2 the aircraft was primarily flown by Col. Shower and Lt. Col. Mahoney. Unlike the first Little Pete this aircraft was still a thoroughbred fighter as it retained armament and a gunsight.

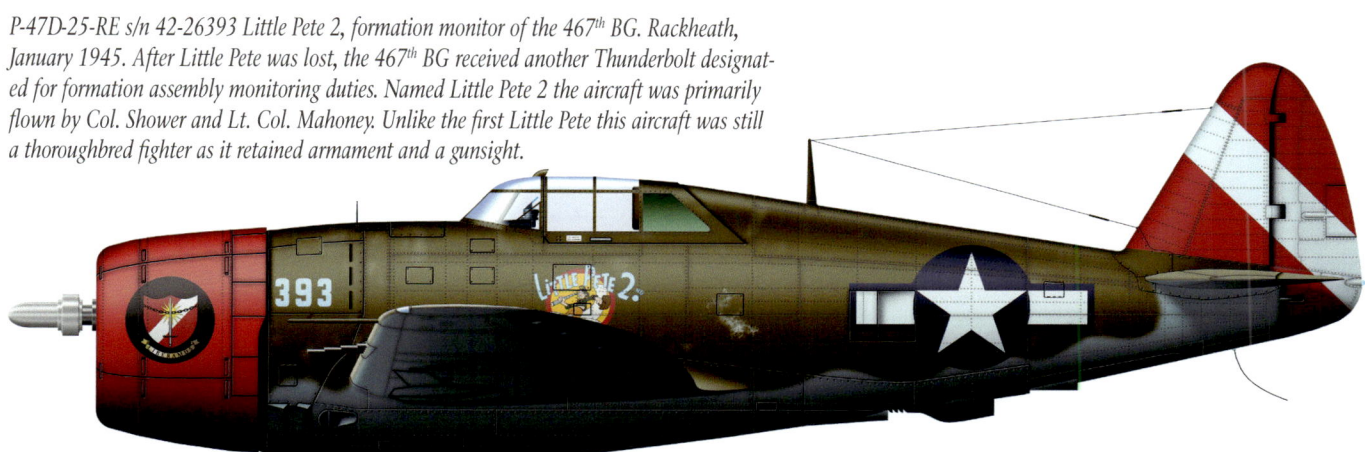

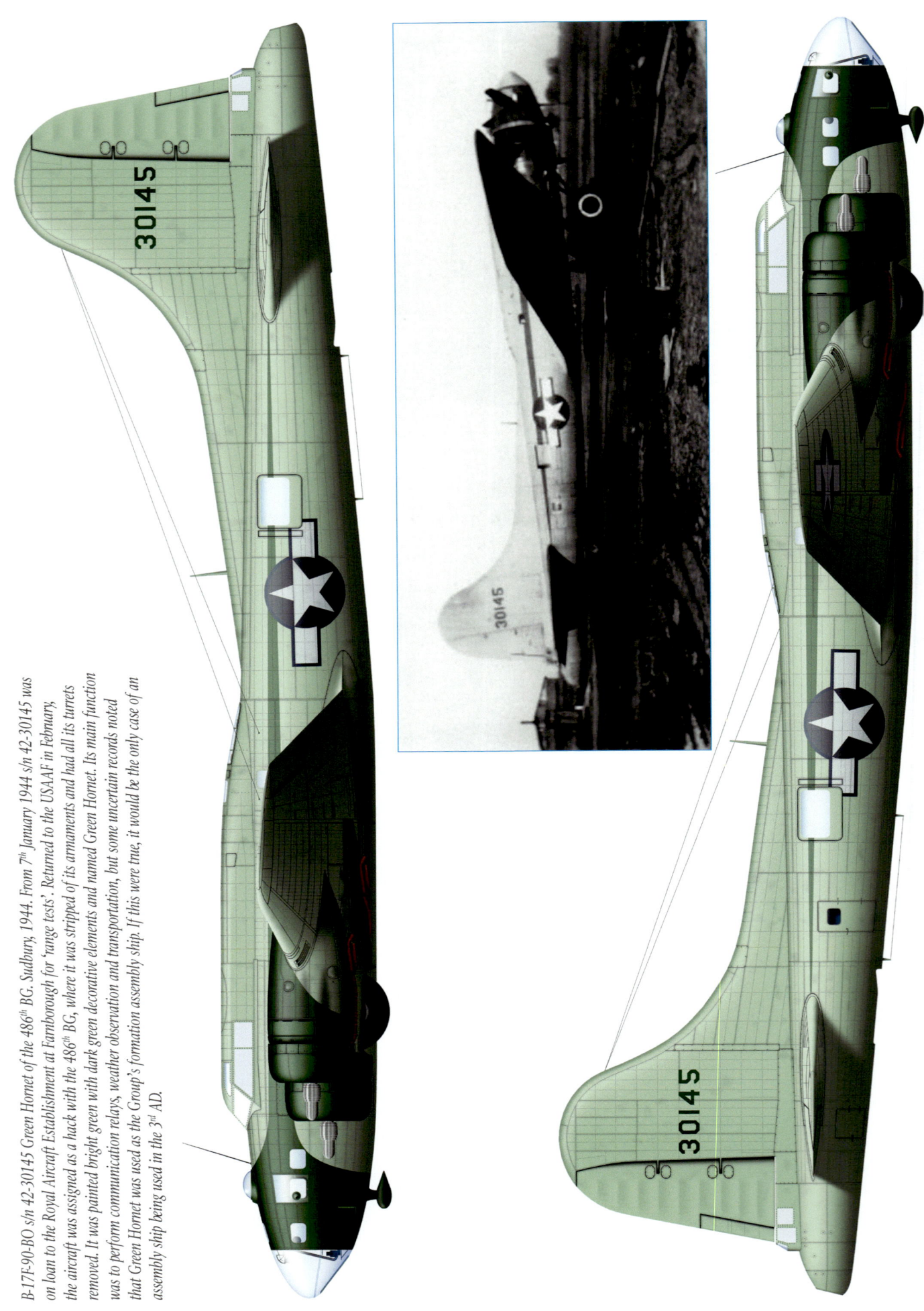

B-17F-90-BO s/n 42-30145 Green Hornet of the 486th BG, Sudbury, 1944. From 7th January 1944 s/n 42-30145 was on loan to the Royal Aircraft Establishment at Farnborough for 'range tests'. Returned to the USAAF in February, the aircraft was assigned as a hack with the 486th BG, where it was stripped of its armaments and had all its turrets removed. It was painted bright green with dark green decorative elements and named Green Hornet. Its main function was to perform communication relays, weather observation and transportation, but some uncertain records noted that Green Hornet was used as the Group's formation assembly ship. If this were true, it would be the only case of an assembly ship being used in the 3rd AD.

P-47D-6-RE s/n 42-74680 of the 486th BG. Sudbury, March 1945. Originally s/n 42-74680 served in the 352nd FS / 353rd FG at Raydon where it was given the code SX●I. Declared war-weary it was withdrawn from combat use and assigned for second-line duties. It was transferred to the 486th BG, and was used as a formation monitor.

P-47C-2-RE #41-6271 *Rat Racer*, a formation monitor of the 490th Bomb Group. Eye, spring of 1945. All markings of the previous user (the 56th FG code HV•Z) were overpainted with the exception of the 'Rat Racer' artwork. The serial was re-marked lower down as 16271WW.

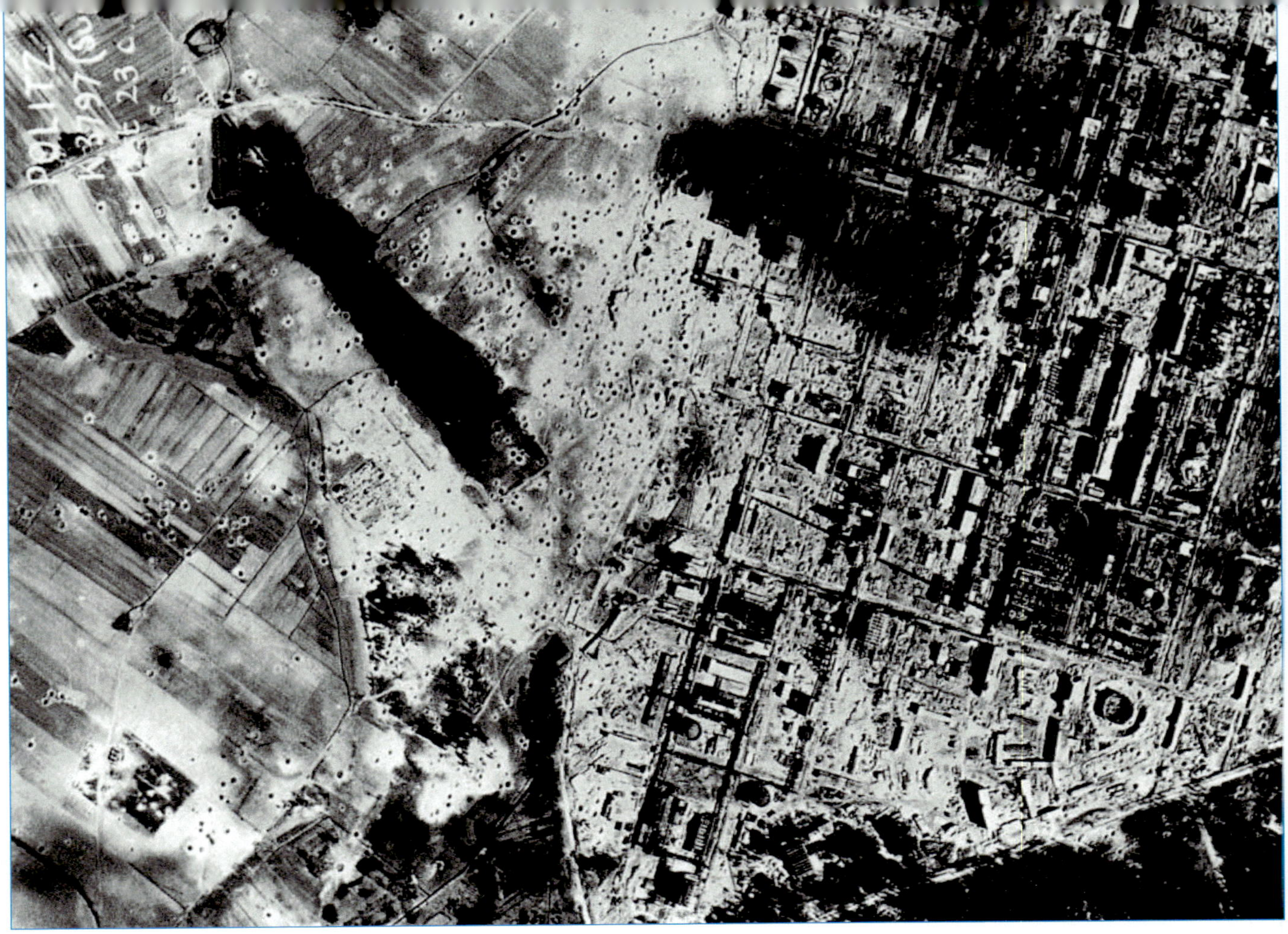

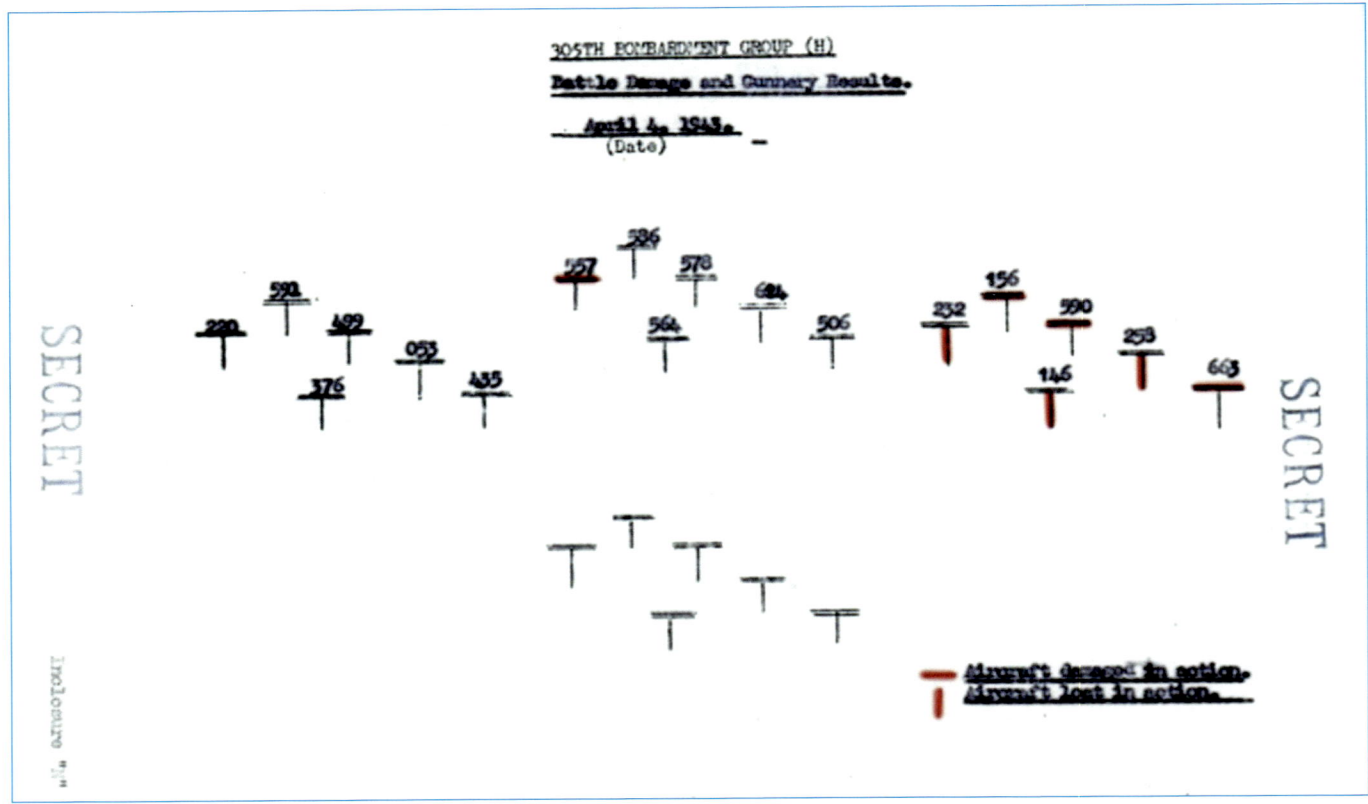

After the battle: balance of losses and benefits: Politz Oil Refinery photo taken by a photo-reconnaissance aircraft after an American bombing raid on 3rd March 1945 (above); a typical form enclosed with a report, which showed in a simple graphic form the losses (statistics) after a mission of the 305th BG on 4th April 1943 (below).

SECRET

305TH BOMBARDMENT GROUP (H)

Battle Damage and Gunnery Results.

April 4, 1943.
(Date)

220 591 499 376 053 435 557 586 578 564 684 506 232 156 590 146 258 663

Aircraft damaged in action.
Aircraft lost in action.

Inclosure

SECRET

I would like to thank all the people who have been helping me in my researches or assisted in any other way, especially Richard Franks, Will Lundy, Paul Wilson, Bill Davenport, Ken Harbour, Andy Wilkinson, Rod Hupp, Wallace Blackwell, Geoff Ward, Michael Faley, Irv Baum, and last but not the least Adam Jarski.